D1706801

About the author

Ph.D. in Information and Knowledge Engineering from the University of Alcalá de Henares. Master of Educational Planning and Management from Universidad Galileo and Master in Production and Management of e-Learning Projects from Universidad Carlos III de Madrid (UC3M), Spain. Senior researcher in the field of education with a focus on MOOCs, artificial intelligence in education, STEAM, and micro-credentials. Innovative educational technology project consultant. Expert in digital education.

Author and coordinator of the courses at edX platform: "Unlocking the Power of Generative AI with ChatGPT for Higher Education", "Artificial Intelligence Tools for Productivity: Beyond ChatGPT", "Intro to AI for Digital Marketing," "AI Technology for Marketing Optimization," and "AI for Marketing Strategy and Creativity." Consultant in Generative AI and AI-driven Chatbot solutions. Dedicated trainer in cutting-edge Generative AI tools.

© Miguel Morales-Chan Ph.D

PREFACE

As I delved into ChatGPT's capabilities, I learned invaluable techniques to optimize its efficacy. I found that the key lies in employing specific language and focusing on clear objectives to yield accurate and useful outcomes. With each interaction, my understanding of how to productively engage with ChatGPT expanded, enabling me to unlock its full potential. It has been a rewarding experience, and I am eager to share my insights with you.

In this book, you will learn how to effectively and creatively interact with ChatGPT to obtain extraordinary and pertinent responses in the educational field. We will explore everything you need to know about ChatGPT for curriculum design, learning planning, educational material creation, learning activity design, and assessments, all using real-world examples and best practices. This course will equip you with the necessary skills to master the art of creating teaching-focused prompts. You will receive teaching-focused prompts along with 90 highly customizable and specific templates, empowering you to create superior educational content.

Prompt templates will provide you with a solid and coherent structure for your interactions with the tool. This implies that you won't need to initiate a conversation with ChatGPT every time; instead, you can customize each template by simply replacing the bracketed parameters to suit your unique requirements. This will save you time and effort, allowing you to focus on the content and direction of the conversation rather than the elaboration of prompts.

TABLE OF CONTENTS

© Copyright
All rights reserved.

Total or partial reproduction of this book is prohibited without written permission of the author.

1. INTRODUCTION

1.1 WHAT IS CHATGPT?

OpenAI developed ChatGPT, an artificial intelligence language model. Natural language processing techniques operate it, training it on a vast corpus of web text to generate responses to user-provided questions or prompts. The GPT-3.5 family, regarded as one of the most advanced language models to date, serves as the foundation for ChatGPT. Thanks to machine learning, large language models like ChatGPT can perform various tasks such as summarizing, expanding information, translating texts, making predictions, scripting, coding, and generating speeches with high accuracy.

To use ChatGPT, you simply need to visit OpenAI's website https://chat.openai.com and create a free account. Once you log in, you can begin to interact with the artificial intelligence using a chat bar, which you can use to ask questions, request information, or hold a conversation in any language. Each message you send will be recorded and used to further train the ChatGPT model, improving its ability to interact with users

1.2 CHATGPT AND ITS LIMITATIONS

The use of ChatGPT has become increasingly popular in recent months due to its ability to generate new content by responding to questions and naturally following up on conversations.

However, as with any technology, it is important to consider its limitations and characteristics before using it. The phrase 'all that glitters is not gold' serves as a reminder that not everything that appears to be good or valuable actually is. This adage applies perfectly to ChatGPT, as although it can be a useful tool for quickly generating content, it also has its limitations. One of the major issues with ChatGPT is that, while it is capable of producing coherent and sometimes astonishing responses, these can occasionally be neither accurate nor reliable. The lack of context and the limited nature of the training can lead to incorrect or inappropriate answers. Therefore, it is crucial to always verify the accuracy of ChatGPT's responses before utilizing them.

Additionally, it is important to note that ChatGPT was trained on a large volume of texts, yet it may still be limited in terms of its ability to understand and respond to complex questions. This means that, although it may be useful for simple tasks such as grammatical correction or text-to-emoji conversion, it may not be the best option for more complex tasks. In summary, while ChatGPT can be a useful tool for certain tasks, it is important to be aware of its limitations and to use it cautiously. The phrase 'all that glitters is not gold' reminds us that it is crucial to be critical of technology and to ensure that we are using it effectively and responsibly. Other Limitations:

* *Limitations in Training Data *This limitation is removed with the paid version (ChatGPT 4.0) as it is connected to the internet*
* *Issues of Bias (may lead to insensitive or offensive responses)*
* *Linguistic Limitations (primarily trained in English, and its performance in other languages may be limited)*
* *Lack of Contextual Understanding (may struggle to understand context and maintain coherence in a conversation)*
* *Lack of Deep Understanding on Ethical and Moral Issues*

1.3 THE IMPORTANCE OF PROMPTS

Prompts are phrases or questions used to direct a language model, such as ChatGPT, to produce a response. The quality of the prompts is one of the most important factors for achieving a successful conversation in ChatGPT. Well-defined and precise prompts can help guide the conversation effectively, ensuring that the user's topics of interest are addressed. On the other hand, poorly defined prompts can generate unfocused and unproductive conversations, resulting in a less engaging and informative experience. Therefore, it is crucial to pay attention to the quality of the prompts and ensure that they are well-constructed to achieve a successful conversation in ChatGPT.

When interacting with ChatGPT, it is essential to provide clear and precise context. A clear and concise message will help ensure that ChatGPT understands the topic or task at hand and is able to generate an appropriate response. It is important to be specific when formulating questions, avoiding vague or confusing questions that may generate imprecise responses. Artificial intelligence is only as good as the information provided to it, so it is crucial to provide an appropriate framework for it to deliver a precise and relevant response. In summary, prompts should include: (a) topic, (b) style, (c) tone, (d) context, and (e) contextual information.

Below, I share ten initial recommendations that you should consider when interacting with ChatGPT:

1. **Define a Clear Objective:** Decide what you want ChatGPT to achieve through the message. Whether it is to provide information, guide the conversation, or solve a problem. If your question is vague, your answer will also be vague.

2. **Keep the Message Concise:** Be as concise as possible in your instructions, avoiding unnecessary words. This will help ensure that ChatGPT is able to generate a focused and relevant response.

3. **Use Natural Language:** Write the prompt in an easy-to-understand manner and use everyday language. This helps Chat GPT understand the context and respond appropriately.

4. **Avoid Ambiguity:** Make sure the prompt is specific and avoid ambiguity. Avoid using words with multiple meanings or phrases that could be interpreted in different ways. If you start to get a result you don't like, stop and rephrase your message.

5. **Provide Context:** Offer sufficient context so that ChatGPT understands the conversation's framework and can respond accordingly. If you have multiple instructions but are unsure if Chat GPT understands them, you can ask it to analyze your prompt. Add any other aspects you consider important.

6. **Avoid Open-Ended Questions:** Do not pose questions without a clear answer. This can generate irrelevant or confusing responses from ChatGPT. Instead, try to be as specific as possible in your questions, defining a clear purpose and focus for the conversation.

7. **Consider Tone and Language Used in the Conversation:** To maintain a meaningful and engaging conversation, it is important to consider the tone and language used. Avoid using overly informal or derogatory language, as this can break down communication. Instead, aim for a respectful and professional tone, using a clear and easily understandable dialogue.

8. **Use Specific Words and Phrases to Guide the Outcome:** For example, if you want ChatGPT to generate a humorous story, you can include words like "funny" or "laughter" in the prompt.

9. **Define Jargon or Technical Terms:** If you need to use jargon or technical terms in your messages, make sure to provide clear definitions or explanations for these terms. This way, both ChatGPT and the user will be on the same page, avoiding misunderstandings.

10. **Review and Revise Your Message:** Make sure to take a moment to review the message and verify that it is easy to understand. It is important to consider whether the language used is specific and relevant to the topic of the conversation, and whether the message is focused and clear, leaving no room for ambiguities. This careful review can help ensure that the message is adequately conveyed to ChatGPT, increasing the likelihood of receiving a satisfactory response.

"A GOOD CONVERSATION WITH CHATGPT CAN LEAD YOU TO ACHIEVE SURPRISING RESULTS AND DISCOVER SOLUTIONS YOU WOULD HAVE NEVER IMAGINED."

Verbs are the engine of artificial intelligence, as they are action words that guide the direction and structure of the AI, allowing it to know which actions to take and what information to provide. In this regard, using the correct verbs in the prompts given to the AI can make a difference in the accuracy and relevance of the responses obtained. For example, if the verb 'analyze' is used to instruct the AI to examine a data set, a more detailed and precise response can be obtained than if a generic verb like 'look' is used.

Likewise, by using specific and focused verbs, one can request precise tasks from the AI, such as explaining concepts or generating ideas, resulting in more accurate and focused responses. Ultimately, choosing the appropriate verb in a prompt is key to ensuring that the AI understands what is being asked of it and provides relevant and accurate answers, which can have a significant impact on the quality of the solutions and recommendations it offers. Below, I present a list of verbs you might consider using when interacting with ChatGPT:

Clarify	Argue	Change	Combine
Compile	Verify	Conclude	Compare
Create	Criticize	Defend	Define
Describe	Differentiate	Expand	Explain
Generate	Make	Illustrate	Include
Infer	List	Provide	Produce
Propose	Recommend	Summarize	Rethink

The tone of voice in prompts is also essential in the educational realm. Educators can benefit from choosing a consistent and appropriate tone for their prompts, as this can strengthen the relationship with students, build trust, and increase their motivation. Teachers can employ different tones depending on the task at hand, such as a more formal and academic tone for the presentation of a complex subject, a more friendly and personalized tone for individual feedback, or a more playful and engaging tone for an educational game.

Accesible	Friendly	Happy	Alluring

Assertive	Attractive	Casual	Científico
Detailed	Educational	Eloquent	Empático
Enthusiastic	Formal	Informative	Inspirador
Motivational	Informal	Useful	Personal
Melancholic	Neutral	Respectful	Technical
Professional	Reflective	Valuation	Solidarity

1. 4 EFECTIVE PROMPTS

The importance of well-crafted prompts in interacting with ChatGPT cannot be overstated. A high-quality prompt should consider several elements: the role of ChatGPT, a clear objective, context, and clear examples or characteristics of the desired output format. When ChatGPT takes on role-playing, such as acting as an expert in digital education topics, it can generate highly specialized content or advice. For instance, a teacher could prompt ChatGPT with 'Act as an expert in digital education and provide strategies for improving student engagement in online classes.' This would guide the AI to produce a comprehensive guide on best practices for online pedagogy or offer specific strategies for student engagement in a virtual classroom. This role-based interaction underscores the essence of the principle that 'the more information in your prompt, the better the output will be.' Employing 'few-shot learning' by providing examples can guide the AI in generating more accurate and contextually relevant responses. Additionally, if the conversation requires elaboration or exceeds the 1,000-character limit of ChatGPT, a 'chain of thought' approach can be employed by writing multiple prompts within the same conversation, allowing for a more nuanced and detailed interaction.

Given that crafting high-quality prompts can be time-consuming, it is advisable to invest time in prompts that can be reused across various educational scenarios. Iteration is often necessary to fine-tune these prompts for optimal results. The time spent on this task is an investment in the educational process, as it significantly impacts the AI's ability to generate solutions, recommendations, or educational content that is both precise and relevant. In summary, the quality of the prompt directly correlates with the quality of the output, making it a critical factor in the effective utilization of AI in educational settings. There are different types of prompts that can be used with ChatGPT, each with its own focus and objective. Below, I present a series of examples oriented towards the Educational Field.

(a) Sequential: Sequential prompts are those that seek to create a logical progression in the conversation with ChatGPT, using a sequence of previous texts to obtain a coherent and precise response. Suggested structure: **Prompt [A] + Prompt [B] = Prompt [C]**
For example:

* *Prompt: "Describe the evolution of education over the last 50 years and how it has influenced educational innovation."*
* *Prompt: "Mention two examples of innovative technologies that have transformed education and explain how they work."*
* *Prompt: "Now write a short article on the evolution of education over the last 50 years and include the two examples of innovative technologies that have transformed education"*

(b) Conditional: Conditional prompts ask ChatGPT to generate text based on a condition or assumption. Suggested structure: **If [condition] + question [topic] + for [objective]**

For example:

* Prompt: "If technology is used appropriately in the classroom, what impact could it have on educational innovation to enhance student learning?"
* Prompt: "If personalized learning is widely adopted in the future, how could it change the classroom dynamics and improve student performance to achieve more effective education?"

(c) Comparative: Comparative prompts ask ChatGPT to compare two or more things and/or situations, thereby obtaining more specific results. **Suggested structure: Compare question 1 [topic 1] and question 2 [topic 2].**
For example:

* Prompt: "Compare the effectiveness of online education with face-to-face education in terms of learning and motivation."
* Prompt: "Compare and contrast two innovative teaching methods and explain which is more effective and why."

(d) Argumentative: Argumentative prompts are those that seek for ChatGPT to generate a clear and coherent argument or position on a particular topic. These prompts are typically structured as a direct request to the AI to argue for or against an idea, using information provided earlier. **Suggested structure: Argue + [topic] + for [outcome].**
For example:

* Prompt: "Argue why it is important to implement educational innovation today."
* Prompt: "Argue against online education and explain why face-to-face education remains the most effective option."

(e) Professional Perspective: This type of prompt asks ChatGPT to assume the role of a specific person and describe a topic in a given context, such as if it were a narrator or a journalist. This can help make the response more detailed, objective, and structured, and can also provide a different focus in the answer.

Suggested structure: Act + as [author or profession] + and describe [topic] + context.
For example:

✳ *Prompt: "Act as an educational innovation consultant and describe how you would approach the implementation of technology in a school in the context of a pandemic."*
✳ *Prompt: "Act as a teacher who is an expert in educational technology and describe how you would incorporate innovative teaching methods in your classroom to foster autonomous learning in students."*

(f) **Wishlist:** This is a structure that helps users get more specific and relevant answers from ChatGPT by providing a list of specific requirements they wish to meet. By providing this list, the user is giving detailed information about their needs and preferences, allowing ChatGPT to provide a more accurate and focused response. **Suggested structure: I am looking for [option/object/solution] with [requirement 1], [requirement 2], and [requirement 3].**
For example:

✳ *Prompt: "I am looking for an innovative solution to improve student engagement in my online classes. I would like to include the use of gamification tools in my class, track student progress, and have the ability to customize content. Could you recommend some application examples that meet these requirements?"*

1.5 CHATGPT'S ROLE IN THE TEACHING PROCESS

From the perspective of the educator, ChatGPT offers multiple opportunities to enhance the quality of teaching. Firstly, it can serve as a tool to broaden the scope of education, allowing students to access a wealth of information and online resources. This means that students can have access to detailed answers and explanations on specific topics at any time and from anywhere, enabling them to progress at their own pace.

Furthermore, ChatGPT can be employed as a tool to improve learning feedback. By generating coherent and relevant responses to students' questions, educators can utilize this technology to offer instant and personalized feedback. This aids students in better understanding concepts, correcting mistakes, and enhancing their academic performance.

Another opportunity presented by ChatGPT is the potential for personalized education and learning. Through the identification of patterns in students' performance, ChatGPT can generate specific responses and resources for each student, allowing them to address problem areas and improve their understanding of topics. However, the presence of artificial intelligence raises questions about our educational and evaluative processes. University assessment often involves students submitting products of their learning for grading, such as essays or written assignments. However, AI systems can generate these products more efficiently and with higher quality in less time and with minimal effort on the part of the student. This means that the products submitted by students can no longer provide authentic and reliable evidence of their performance and achievement of course outcomes.

Artificial intelligence systems, like ChatGPT, have the potential to revolutionize teaching and assessment in the classroom. By employing this tool to foster discussions, provide personalized feedback, and enhance linguistic and literacy skills, educators can create a more engaging and effective learning environment for their students.

In the following section, I present a series of instructional proposals for ChatGPT from the perspective of "Teaching": (a) Curriculum Design, (b) Learning Planning, (c) Generation of Educational Materials, (d) Design of Learning Activities, and (e) Design of Assessments.

2. IMPLEMENTING CHAT GPT IN EDUCATIONAL PLANNING

Curriculum design is a fundamental process that involves various actions aimed at planning and structuring the content and teaching methodology for a course or educational program. Some of the actions carried out during curriculum design include identifying the content and learning objectives, defining teaching and assessment methods, designing units and lessons, and adjusting and reviewing the curriculum, among others. In this section, we will explore how ChatGPT can help save valuable time by streamline the process of defining learning objectives, designing content units and lessons, as well as determining the most appropriate teaching and assessment methods.

"CURRICULUM DESIGN IS THE HEART OF THE EDUCATIONAL PROCESS, AS IT IS THE MEANS BY WHICH WHAT IS TAUGHT, HOW IT IS

TAUGHT, AND HOW STUDENT LEARNING IS ASSESSED AND DEFINED."

2.1 LEARNING OBJECTIVES AND COMPETENCIES

Learning objectives are specific and measurable goals that a student is expected to achieve during a teaching process. These objectives describe what a student should know or be able to do at the end of a course or a particular learning activity.

Learning objectives help define expected outcomes and guide the development of teaching content and activities. Additionally, learning objectives are a valuable tool for assessment, as they allow for determining whether students have achieved the expected outcomes and whether the course or activity has been effective. Below, I present some ideas for prompts:

#1 Define Learning Objectives	
Objective	*Obtain generic ideas for learning objectives of a course*
Template	*Write [number] learning objectives for a course on [course topic]*
Prompt	*Write 5 learning objectives for a course on the topic of Educational Innovation.*

If we wish to enhance our outcomes, it is essential to consider the recommendations provided in sections 1.3 and 1.4. Keep in mind that well-defined and precise prompts can effectively guide the conversation, ensuring that the user's topics of interest are addressed. Below, I present an alternative prompt aimed at improving results would be:

#2 Draft Learning Objectives using Booms Taxonomy	
Objective	*Draft learning objectives for a course, taking into account the six cognitive levels of Bloom's Taxonomy: remember, understand, apply, analyze, evaluate, and create.*
Template	*Generate a learning objective using Bloom's Taxonomy for the [cognitive level] level of cognition, related to [study theme], that includes a performance criterion demonstrating the ability to apply educational innovation concepts and tools in a specific project. Use the following structure [action verb]+[cognitive level]+ [context]+[performance criteria].*
Prompt	*Generate a learning objective using Bloom's Taxonomy for the 'create' level of cognition, related to the theme of 'Educational Innovation,' that includes a performance criterion demonstrating the ability to apply educational innovation concepts and tools in a specific project. Use the following structure [Action Verb] + [Cognitive Level] + [Context] + [Performance Criteria].*

A more effective instruction might be considering an expert role:

#3 Draft Learning Objectives as an Expert	
Objective	*Draft learning objectives for a course from an expert's perspective. This type of instruction could help obtain a more detailed, objective, and structured response.*
Template	*Act as [role or profession] and draft [number, expected outcome] for the course [course theme] [context].*
Prompt	*Act as an expert in 'educational innovation topics' and write 2 learning objectives for the course 'Educational Innovation' which will have master's level students as participants.*

For instance, here's an instruction to compare the obtained results to evaluation criteria like their writing style and their measurable and achievable nature:

#4 Evaluate the Defined Learning Objectives	
Objective	*Compare learning objectives with previously defined evaluation criteria.*
Template	*Compare the previously proposed learning objectives based on the following criteria: [criterion 1], [criterion 2], [criterion 3].*
Prompt	*Compare the previously proposed learning objectives based on the following criteria: (a) must be clearly defined, (b) measurable, and (c) achievable.*

In the curriculum design process, competencies are defined with the goal of establishing the skills and abilities that students are expected to acquire upon completing the course or educational program. A competency is a skill or capability that the student must possess, demonstrate, or apply in practical or real situations.

#5 Writing competencies	
Objective	*Writing course competencies taking into account the structure "[INFINITIVE VERB + CONCEPTUAL OBJECT] + [PURPOSE] + [CONDITION OF REFERENCE] + [FORM OF APPROPRIATION]"*
Template	*Write [number] course competencies [course subject matter] using the [desired structure].*
Prompt	*"Write 3 competencies from the course "Educational Innovation", using this structure: [INFINITIVE VERB + CONCEPTUAL OBJECT] + [PURPOSE] + [REFERENCE CONDITION] + [APPROPRIATE FORM]."*

2. 2 CREATION OF CONTENT AGENDA

Determine the key topics that must be covered to achieve each defined learning objective and/or competency. A core instruction could be for example:

#6 Define a content agenda	
Objective	*Obtain generic ideas for content agenda*
Template	*Create an outline of the topics to be covered in a course on the [course subject] + [context].*
Prompt	*"Create an outline of the topics to be covered in a course on the subject of "Educational Innovation", to be taught at the master's level.*

An instruction referring to the results obtained in the previous interactions would be for example:

#7 Define a content agenda based on previous results.	
Objective	*Obtain a detailed outline of the topics for the content agenda, taking previous interactions as a reference.*
Template	*Generates a detailed summary of the topics to be included in the content agenda of a course on [course topic] + based on [previous results] + [context].*
Prompt	*"Generate a detailed summary of the topics that should be included in the content agenda of a course on the subject "Educational Innovation", based on the "learning objectives" defined above." You should take into account that it will be for graduate level students and will have a duration of 4 weeks of study."*

More specific instruction may be useful in defining the sub-contents of a lesson study, based on a competency or learning objective.

#8 Defining a sub-content agenda for a lesson	
Objective	*Generate a detailed outline of sub-content topics for a lesson, taking as a reference the defined learning objectives.*
Template	*Generate a detailed summary of the topics to be covered in the lesson [lesson name], covering the [learning objective]. + [context]*
Prompt	*"Generate a detailed summary of the topics to be covered in the lesson "Web 2.0 Tools, which covers the learning objective "Upon completion of this course, students will be able to use web 2.0 tools to effectively create and share online content." You should note that it will be for graduate level students and will have a duration of 1 week of study."*

A more detailed instruction, which takes into account the logical order of presentation of the contents, takes as a reference a list of requirements and respects a format, could be for example:

#9 Define an agenda of contents taking into account the logical ord	
Objective	*Obtain a detailed outline of the topics for the content agenda, considering the logical order of presentation of the contents.*
Template	*Organize the topics and sub-topics of a syllabus for a course on [specific topic] in a logical and coherent order.*
Prompt	*Organize the topics and sub-topics of an agenda for a course on "Academic Integrity" in a logical and coherent order.*

#10 Define a content agenda from a list of contents	
Objective	*Obtain generic ideas for content syllabus from a list of desired features or specifications for the syllabus.*
Template	*Generate a course content syllabus for the [course topic] course with the following requirements: [insert here a list of desired features or specifications for the syllabus].*

Prompt	*"Generate a content syllabus for the "Educational Innovation" course with the following requirements: The agenda must include at least 8 topics related to the importance of technology in education, each topic must be at least 1.5 hours long and the agenda must be designed for a graduate level."*

#11 Define an agenda of contents based on a format	
Objective	*Obtain generic ideas for a content agenda from a specific format.*
Template	*Write a content syllabus on the [course topic] following this format: [insert here an example of the format you would like the syllabus to have, e.g. introduction, objectives, contents, conclusions, etc.].*
Prompt	*"Write a content agenda on the topic "Educational Innovation" following this format: The agenda should include an introduction, learning objectives, content, learning activities, and conclusions."*

2.3 CREATION OF COURSE DESCRIPTION

The course outline provides a broad overview of the course's scope, emphasizing the learning objectives and/or competencies, the content schedule, and the study methods, among other elements. For example, a specific instruction might have the following structure:

#12 Create a course description	
Objective	*Obtain generic ideas for the general description of a course.*
Template	*Prepare a general description describing the course [subject of the course] in detail, including [additional information or details required e.g. methodology or mode of study, duration, focus, level, etc.].*

Prompt	*"Prepare an overview that describes the Educational Innovation course in detail, including course duration, mode of study, and necessary prerequisites."*

2.4 COURSE PROGRAM CREATION

A course syllabus is a document that describes the learning objectives, contents, teaching methods, evaluation criteria and other relevant aspects of a course. In general, it is used to plan and design a course in a coherent and structured manner. A specific instruction would have the following structure for example:

#13 Propose a course program	
Objective	*Generate proposals for a course program*
Template	*Create a course syllabus that addresses the topic of the [course topic]. Consider + [the learning objectives]+[the syllabus]+[the course description] + including. Be sure to justify the inclusion of each of the topics and learning activities and their relevance to the development of the skills and competencies sought in the learners.*
Prompt	*"Create a course syllabus that addresses the topic of educational innovation. Consider the main concepts and topics to be covered in the course, as well as the activities and teaching methodologies to be used. Be sure to justify the inclusion of each of the topics and activities, and their relevance to the development of the skills and competencies sought in the students."*

NOTE: To achieve the best results, you may ask ChatGPT to first define the exit profile, learning objectives, content agenda, and course description. Then, based on the learning outcomes, it can generate the course syllabus proposal.

3. OPTIMIZING LEARNING PLANNING

Learning planning is essential to ensure that students receive a quality education and achieve their learning objectives. In learning planning, teachers can set clear objectives, define the content that should be taught, identify the most effective teaching methods and strategies, and determine the best way to assess student progress. Planning also allows teachers to adapt their teaching to the needs and abilities of students, and ensure that all students receive equitable education. In summary, learning planning is a fundamental part of the educational process and can help ensure that students reach their maximum potential and improve the utilization of technology integration in the teaching and learning process.

"LEARNING PLANNING IS KEY TO EDUCATIONAL SUCCESS, AS IT ALLOWS FOR SETTING CLEAR OBJECTIVES AND EFFECTIVE STRATEGIES TO ACHIEVE THEM"

3.1 CREATION OF A LESSON PLAN

In every class session, before students arrive, teachers must decide what activities, tasks, and discussions would be effective in a given topic. Writing lesson plans is something teachers do all the time and it takes a substantial amount of time and effort to create them. Here are a number of examples of how to use ChatGPT.

#14 Create a lesson plan	
Objective	*Obtain generic ideas for lesson planning.*
Template	*Prepares a lesson plan on [the desired topic] that allows establishing [clear objectives, defining the contents to be taught, identifying the most effective teaching methods and strategies, and determining the best way to evaluate students' progress], taking into consideration the [characteristics of the target audience]+ [context].*
Prompt	*"Prepare a lesson plan on the topic "The role of the teacher in context of educational innovation", which allows to establish clear objectives, define the contents to be taught, identify the most effective teaching methods and strategies, and determine the best way to evaluate the students' progress" takes into account that the students are graduate level and the class has a duration of 60 minutes."*

If you want better results, ask for suggestions for the development of specific activities within the class period, for example:

#15 Create a proposal of practical activities for the class	
Objective	*Obtain generic ideas for the development of practical activities that can be carried out during a class session.*
Template	*Imagine you are an [author or profession] + who wishes to further [learning objective]. Provide three ideas of practical activities you could do in [study mode] to achieve this objective.*
Prompt	*"Imagine you are an expert teacher in Educational Innovation who wishes to foster students' understanding of the role of the teacher in context of educational innovation. Provide three ideas for practical activities that you could do in class to achieve this goal."*

Another aspect in which ChatGPT can support you is by generating ideas on how to approach or present a specific topic. You may be asked to share "application scenarios", "trend analysis", "relevant statistics and data" or "metaphors and analogies", as well as supporting "bibliographic references", in order to have relevant information to support the class development.

#16 Create a proposal to address a topic with scenarios	
Objective	*Obtain generic ideas of application scenarios to be used in the development of a topic.*
Template	*Pose an application scenario + to address the [topic of study] + [context]. Give me [characteristics of the type of response desired].*
Prompt	*"Pose an application scenario to address the topic "the importance of feedback" with my graduate students in the "Educational Innovation" course. Give me details on how to start with the development of the topic, providing innovative examples."*

With the following prompt, you can ask ChatGPT to provide you with information about the latest trends in educational technology and how they are being applied in the context of educational innovation. In addition, you are asking ChatGPT to provide suggestions on how these trends could be used in innovative ways to foster student creativity. ChatGPT's response could include specific examples of how these trends are being used and how they could be applied to foster student creativity.

#17 Create a proposal to address a trending topic	
Objective	*Obtain a list of trends to address a topic of study in class.*

Template	(a) Provide a list of recent trends or advances in the area of [topic of study] and suggest how these could be used to develop an innovative approach to the analysis of this topic.
	(b) Describe the most relevant trends in [topic of study] and how they might influence its future development. Provide 5 suggestions on how we might use this information to approach the topic in an innovative way.
Prompt 1	"Pose an application scenario to address the topic "the importance of feedback" with my graduate students in the "Educational Innovation" course. Give me details on how to start with the development of the topic, providing innovative examples."
Prompt 2	"In the context of educational innovation, how are the latest trends in educational technology being applied and how could they be used in innovative ways to foster student creativity?"

Next, I present an example of requesting ChatGPT to provide ideas for metaphors and/or analogies to explain a concept. You could then use these metaphors and/or analogies in a practical exercise, such as a role-playing game or a team-building activity, to promote students' understanding and application of the concept.

#18 Create a proposal to address a topic with metaphors.	
Objective	Obtain ideas from metaphors and/or analogies for the development of a topic of study.
Template	What metaphors and/or analogies could be used to explain [the concept or theme] ? How could these metaphors and/or analogies be used in a [type of activity] to promote [the didactic objective] + [context]?

Prompt	*"What metaphors and/or analogies could be used to explain the concept of collaborative learning? How could these metaphors and/or analogies be used in a practical exercise to foster student understanding and application of the concept?"*

When presenting a specific topic, it's always important to have reliable and up-to-date sources that serve as a reference and help deepen our understanding of the subject. In this regard, having an appropriate selection of bibliographic references can be key to the success of our work. Fortunately, with the help of ChatGPT, we can access a wide variety of resources and references. If you need a specific reference on a particular topic, you can use the following prompt to request ChatGPT's support in finding information.

#19 Identify bibliographic references	
Objective	*Obtain bibliographic references to address a topic of study.*
Template	*(a) Could you provide me with some bibliographic references on [specific topic] that are relevant to [type of audience]?* *(b) Could you suggest some bibliographic references on [specific topic] that have been published in the last [number of years] years?*
Prompt	*"Could you suggest some literature references on the use of technology in education that have been published in the last 5 years?"*

Today, a wide variety of technological tools are available to support topic presentation in the classroom. These tools may include presentation applications, online platforms, and educational games, among others. A teacher may need to search for and select the tools that best suit his or her teaching objectives and help enrich his or her students' learning experiences.

#20 Identify technology tools to support a topic	
Objective	*Obtain ideas of technological tools that could be useful for the presentation or analysis of a topic of study.*
Template	*What technology tools might be useful for [topic of study] and how can they be used in [specific activity related to the topic]?"*
Prompt	*"What technology tools might be useful in presenting or analyzing the topic of the importance of feedback? Give me at least three specific tools and provide a brief description of how they could be used to enhance students' understanding of the topic.* *For example, how could we use tools such as Mentimeter or Kahoot to encourage student engagement and reflection on feedback? Could we use some video conferencing platform, such as Zoom or Google Meet, to simulate online feedback and discuss its importance in the current context? Are there data analysis tools, such as Excel or Tableau, that could be useful for visualizing and better understanding the impact of feedback on student learning?"*

Using ChatGPT to answer the question "What are the best resources for teaching a specific topic?" can be very useful for teachers when planning their lessons and finding relevant and effective educational materials. The prompts provide a structured guide for identifying the most appropriate resources for each topic, which can save time and effort for teachers in searching for materials. In addition, the prompts can help teachers discover new resources that they may not have known about previously, which can enrich their teaching and improve the learning experience for students. In short, using a prompt to find the best resources for teaching a specific topic can enhance the quality of teaching and learning by ensuring that the educational materials are suitable, relevant, and effective for students.

#21 Provide useful resources for teaching a topic	
Objective	*Provide a list of useful and specific resources for teaching a specific topic.*
Template	*Develop a list of [number] online resources that can be used for [action] the [specific topic], describing [additional information or specific details].*
Prompt	*"Develop a list of 10 online resources (websites, videos, blogs, infographics, among others) that can be used to teach the impact of educational technology, describing highlights and potential classroom applications."*

ChatGPT is a tool that can be used by teachers to generate guidelines for explaining difficult concepts and provide examples. The ability of this tool to generate accurate and relevant text and examples from specific information and questions is promising. By using ChatGPT, teachers can provide a detailed description of a difficult concept, identify problematic areas, and suggest ways to address these challenges.

#22 Provide guidelines to explain difficult concepts	
Objective	*Identify guidelines for explaining difficult concepts and provide me with examples.*
Template	*Generate guidelines to explain the [specific topic] + to [context] and provide [additional information or specific details].*
Prompt 1	*"Generate guidelines to explain the concept of "artificial intelligence" to Ph.D. students and provide some examples to illustrate the concept."*
Prompt 2	*"Provide real-life examples of [physics concept]."*
Prompt 3	*"How can I teach [physics concept] in a more engaging way?"*
Prompt 4	*"What are the different methods for solving [mathematical problem]?"*

Prompt 5	"What are the different formulas used to calculate [physical concept]?"
Prompt 6	"What are the steps to solve [math problem]?"
Prompt 7	"How can I simplify the concept of [topic] for my students?"

Another way to implement ChatGPT is to develop proposals to improve the effectiveness of a synchronous videoconferencing session.

#23 Provide guidelines for effectiveness in synchronous classes.	
Objective	Generate proposals to improve the effectiveness of a synchronous session with videoconferencing.
Template	Generate a list of guidelines to make my synchronous sessions more [context] for the students. Give me some [expected outcomes] on how I can improve my approach and keep students engaged and motivated throughout the session.
Prompt	"Generate a list of guidelines to make my synchronous sessions more effective for the students. Give me some ideas or suggestions on how I can improve my approach and keep students engaged and motivated throughout the session."

3.2 PRESENTATION STRUCTURE OF CLASS (LESSON)

After having established the themes and objectives for the class, we can leverage the capabilities of ChatGPT to gather information and create a structured proposal that facilitates the presentation of the lesson. It is possible to obtain ideas and concepts relevant to the lesson's topics, thus allowing an enrichment in its planning. In short, by using ChatGPT, we can have an effective tool to enrich the planning and presentation of our classes, offering students a more comprehensive and enriching educational experience. A basic instruction could be, for example:

#24 Propose a structure for a lesson presentation	
Objective	Obtain a guide content structure for the development of a presentation.
Template	Generate a presentation structure on [concept or subject matter] + [context].
Prompt	"Generate a presentation structure on the topic: "The role of the teacher in the context of educational innovation" focused on doctoral students".

A more specific instruction, detailing precise features of the presentation, would be for example:

#25 Propose a detailed structure for a presentation	
Objective	Obtain a super detailed content structure for the development of a presentation.
Template	Generate a presentation structure on the topic of [topic]. It includes an introduction that contextualizes the topic, a development that addresses [point 1], [point 2] and [point 3], as well as some concrete strategies for [action]. In addition, include a closing that [action]. Please provide [number] concrete examples and use reliable academic sources to support your ideas.
Prompt	"Generate a presentation structure on the topic of the importance of critical thinking in higher education. Please include an introduction that contextualizes the topic, a development that addresses the benefits and challenges of critical thinking in the classroom, as well as some concrete strategies for fostering it in students. In addition, please include a closing that summarizes key points and promotes reflection and dialogue. Please provide concrete examples and use reliable scholarly sources to support your ideas."

#26 Provide a list of PowerPoint template	
Objective	Get a list of Powerpoint templates for statistical presentation, concrete examples and infographic type images.
Template	Provide a list of creative PowerPoint templates for presenting [type of resource] + about [concept or subject matter] + [context].
Prompt	"Provide a list of creative PowerPoint templates for statistics presentations, concrete examples, and infographic-like images. Provides examples of how they could be used in a presentation on educational technology."

3. 3 IDEAS FOR STARTING YOUR CLASS

The beginning of a class is a crucial moment to establish the dynamics of the session and foster a participatory learning environment. Therefore, it is important to have effective strategies that capture students' attention and motivate their interest in the topic to be discussed. The "Ideas to Start Your Class" prompts are precisely focused on providing teachers with various creative and innovative strategies to achieve this goal and ensure an enriching educational experience. Are you looking for an interesting way to start a class and lack ideas? A basic instruction could be, for example:

#27 Get interesting ideas to start the class	
Objective	Obtain generic ideas to start the class, regardless of the mode of study

Template	(a) Generate some interesting or novel ways to start my [the concept or topic] + [context] class.
	(b) Generate some interesting or novel ideas for starting my next class on [the concept or topic] + [contextualization] + [additional instructions].
Prompt 1	"Generate some interesting or novel ways to start the class "Educational Technology" should be innovative and geared to master's students."
Prompt 2	"Generate some interesting or novel ideas to start my next educational technology class. I would like to find some innovative ways to start the session to capture my students' attention and create a more participatory learning environment.I also need to receive suggestions that are specific to my teaching topic, which is the importance of feedback."

A more specific instruction, requesting a list and detailing some specific characteristics, would be for example:

#28 Obtain a list of ideas to start a class	
Objective	Obtain a list of generic ideas to start the class, regardless of the mode of study.
Template	Generate a list of [number of desired suggestions] forms [adjective description] for [action], including [additional information or specific details].
Prompt	"Generate a list of 5 interesting and novel ways to start a class, including details and concrete examples for each suggestion."

If you are looking for inspiration to create a more engaging and participatory learning experience at the start of your classes, consider the following suggestion:

#29 Provide strategies for an attractive and dynamic classroom	
Objective	*Obtain concrete strategies to start a class in an attractive and dynamic way, regardless of the modality of study.*
Template	*Write [number] + strategies to start a class in [characteristics] + [context].*
Prompt	*"Write 5 strategies for starting a class in an engaging and dynamic way, including details and concrete examples of how they could be implemented."*

Positive and supportive learning environments are characterized as places where students feel safe, supported, and motivated to learn. By using this type of prompt, teachers can identify a range of practical solutions to create a positive and supportive learning environment in the classroom, such as establishing clear and consistent norms, promoting active student participation, providing effective feedback, and paying attention to the diversity and individual needs of students, among others.

The teaching objective when using this type of prompt in the context of creating positive and supportive learning environments is to provide teachers with a list of effective solutions to foster a safe, motivating, and effective environment for student learning.

#30 Encourage the creation of positive learning environments.	
Objective	*Obtain concrete strategies to generate positive and supportive learning environments in the classroom.*
Template	*Generate a list of [number of desired suggestions] ways [adjective description] to [action] a positive and supportive learning environment for your students, including [additional information or specific details].*

Prompt	"Generate a list of 5 effective ways to create a positive and supportive learning environment for your students, including practical examples and helpful recommendations."

Using ChatGPT to answer the question "How can I make a particular topic more engaging for my students?" can be highly useful for teachers in several ways. By providing a list of practical and specific solutions, the prompt can help teachers find new creative ways to teach a topic and make it more interesting for their students.

Additionally, the prompt can also assist teachers in identifying useful multimedia and technological resources that they can use to complement their teaching and make it more attractive and motivating. Ultimately, using a prompt to make a topic more engaging for students can significantly improve the quality of teaching and learning in the classroom, by fostering a more participative, interactive, and entertaining environment for the students.

#31 Ideas for making a given topic more attractive	
Objective	Obtain a list of practical solutions to make a given topic more engaging for students, including specific examples and useful recommendations to apply in the classroom.
Template	Generate a list of [number of desired suggestions] forms [adjective description] for [action], including [additional information or specific details].
Prompt	"Generate a list of examples of how "artificial intelligence" can be applied in everyday situations, including practical examples and clear explanations to help students see the relevance and importance of this topic in their lives."

4. FORMULATING OF CUSTOMIZED DIDACTIC MATERIALS

ChatGPT can assist a teacher in generating educational materials in various ways. As a language model trained across a wide range of fields, it can provide useful information and resources on any subject. For instance, it can be used for generating scripts for podcasts, educational videos, presentations, and other audiovisual teaching resources. Teachers can provide ChatGPT with key points they want to cover in their audiovisual material, and the language model can generate a complete script, including transitions and relevant examples. Additionally, ChatGPT can be used to create mind maps and visual summaries that help students better understand the information. Below, I present a series of examples of its application.

4.1 FORMULATING OF SCRIPTS FOR EDUCATIONAL VIDEOS

Generating scripts for educational videos with the help of ChatGPT can be a valuable tool for enhancing the effectiveness and efficiency of distance learning. With a well-structured and detailed script, teachers can focus their time and energy on presenting content that is relevant and meaningful to students. The use of a script can help ensure that all important points are covered, clear and concise language is used, and active learning is promoted. In summary, using ChatGPT for creating scripts for educational videos can be a valuable tool for improving the quality of distance learning. Below, I present a series of recommendations for teachers who wish to use Chat GPT to generate scripts for educational videos:

* **Make sure to provide clear and precise context:** Before asking ChatGPT to generate a script, ensure you provide detailed and accurate information about the topic and objective of the educational video.
* **Be specific about the structure and tone of the script:** Give ChatGPT a clear idea of how you want the script to be presented, including the structure and tone you desire.
* **Provide additional relevant information:** If you have any additional relevant information that you want included in the script, provide that information to ChatGPT.
* **Review and edit the generated script:** ChatGPT is a powerful tool, but it's important to review and edit the script generated before using it in an educational video.

A basic instruction could be, for example:

#32 Providing a script for an educational video	
Objective	*Obtain a script to generate an educational video*
Template	*Generate a script (script to generate a video) that I will use as support material. The video must present the topic [course topic]+[specific characteristics that the video must have].*
Prompt	*"Generate a script for an educational video that I will use as supporting material. The video should present the topic "Introduction to Educational Technology Research" with a duration of 90 seconds."*

A more detailed instruction would be for example:

#33 Provide a script for a voice-over video	
Objective	Obtain a detailed script to generate a voice-over type educational video.
Template	Generate a script (script to generate a video) of + [specific characteristics that the video should have] + on the [topic]. The audience are graduate students and the tone of voice should be [tone of voice] and should include specific examples. [direct instruction] + [context].
Prompt 1	"Generate a "2 minute" script on "How the TPACK model can support introducing technologies in the classroom". The audience is graduate students and the tone should be serious and motivational should include concrete examples. The video will be voice over type."
Prompt 2	"Generate a "4 minutes" script on "The importance of web 2.0 tools in education". The audience are master's level university students and the structure should be: introduction, basic explanation of the theory, practical applications and conclusion. The video will be voice-over type."

4. 2 PODCAST SCRIPT PRODUCTION

ChatGPT can be a useful tool to support a teacher in creating a script for an educational podcast. By providing a clear and specific prompt that indicates the topic and focus of the podcast, ChatGPT can generate a script structure that includes an engaging introduction, organized sections, and an effective conclusion. In addition, ChatGPT can help include accurate and relevant information about the topic, as well as suggest examples and anecdotes to make the content more interesting and engaging for the audience. By using ChatGPT as a tool, teachers can save time and effort in creating scripts, allowing them to focus on producing and promoting their educational podcast. Below, I show you an example of a basic instruction:

#34 Providing a script for an educational podcast	
Objective	*Obtain a script to generate an educational podcast*
Template	*Pretend to be an expert on the [topic] and give me [number of desired suggestions] to generate a script to generate a podcast on the [topic] + [additional information or specific details].*
Prompt	*"Pretend to be an expert on the topic of Educational Innovation and give me 3 ideas to generate a podcast on the topic "Introduction to Educational Technology Research."*

A more detailed instruction would be for example:

#35 Providing a detailed script for a podcast	
Objective	*Obtain a script to generate a detailed podcast on a topic, taking into account the main characteristics that an educational podcast should have.*
Template	*Generate a script for my podcast on [topic]. I want it to include [starting point] and [ending point], as well as [secondary topics or subtopics to be covered]. The tone of the script should be [formal, informal, humorous, educational, etc.] and the length of the episode will be [X] minutes. Please ensure that the script is well structured and has a clear introduction, a solid development and a coherent conclusion.*
Prompt	*"Generate a script for my podcast on the impact of artificial intelligence on education. I want it to include how artificial intelligence is transforming education, as well as the possible ethical and social implications of this transformation. The tone of the script should be educational and accessible, and the length of the episode will be 20 minutes. Please make sure the script is well-structured and has a clear introduction, a solid development and a coherent conclusion."*

This type of prompt provides ChatGPT with a clear idea of the topic and main points to be covered in the podcast script, as well as the length of the episode and the tone the teacher wishes to be used. In addition, the prompt also calls for a well-defined structure and a coherent introduction, development and conclusion, which will help ensure a clear and organized script for the podcast episode. The use of structured and detailed prompts can help teachers get accurate and useful results from ChatGPT, and ensure that the generated script meets their specific expectations and needs.

4. 3 MIND MAP DEVELOPMENT

As an artificial intelligence language model, ChatGPT does not have the ability to create mind maps, but it can describe an example of how information could be presented. A basic instruction would be for example:

#36 Provide a mind map structure	
Objective	Obtain a structure of a mind map that can be used as a support resource by students.
Template	Act as an expert on the [topic] and give me the structure of a mind map + on the topic [subject of the course. You must [additional information or specific details] + [context].
Prompt 1	"Act as an expert in "Educational Innovation" and give me the structure of a mind map on the topic of "educational technology". It should detail the different levels and relationships. It will be for graduate students for certification in Educational Innovation."
Prompt 2	"Act as a mind map maker and create a map based on the following structure: The main idea or theme, Branches, Keywords, Groupings and Visual support. Use the following information as a basis: [Insert relevant information here]."

ChatGPT can provide you with a basic structure for creating a mind map. From that structure, you can create a mind map using free online tools such as MindMup, Coggle, XMind, among others.

These tools have different features and functionalities, but all of them allow you to create mind maps easily and visually. If you want to illustrate it automatically, we can create the mind map in an online tool, such as Overleaf, which is an online LaTeX editing platform.

First you should generate the structure of the mind map as shown in the previous prompt. With the result obtained, you must ask ChatGPT to generate the LaTeX code, then you will have to copy and paste it into the Overleaf tool and in this way you will have generated the mind map in image mode. Use the following prompt:

#37 Illustrate a mind map from a ChatGPT structure	
Objective	Obtain a graphical illustration/visualization of a mind map from the structure generated by ChatGPT.
Template	Use the [reference] and create the code in Markdown format to illustrate the above mind map. Use [special features].
Prompt	"Generate a proposal to create a mind map on the topic "The Role of the Teacher in Digital Environments", tailored specifically for students enrolled in a MOOC on educational technology.The mind map should aim to explore various facets such as instructional strategies, assessment methods, and ethical considerations. Please submit the mind map in Markdown format."

This prompt will generate a code similar to:

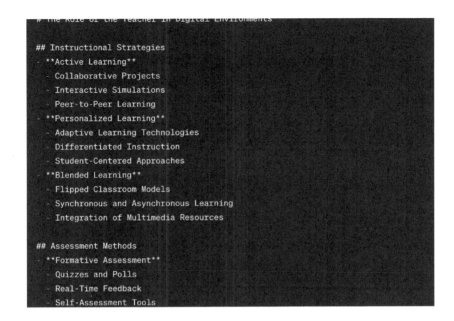

By transferring the code to the Markmaps tool (https://markmap.js.org/) you will get a graphical representation similar to this one:

4.4 DESIGNING INFOGRAPHICS

As an artificial intelligence language model, ChatGPT does not have the ability to create infographics, but it can describe an example of how information could be presented.

#38 Provide a basic structure for an infographic	
Objective	*Obtain a structure and general recommendations for the creation of an infographic on a specific topic.*
Template	*Describe an example of how information on the [topic] could be presented in an infographic + [additional information or specific details] + [context].*
Prompt	*"Describe an example of how information on "issues related to the use of technology in education" could be presented in an infographic, highlighting the most important aspects."*

A more detailed instruction, where the structure, components and graphic styles of an infographic are taken into account, would be for example:

#39 Provide a detailed structure for an infographic	
Objective	*Obtain a detailed structure for the creation of an infographic on a specific topic.*
Template	*Acts as [expert] and creates an infographic, considering the [Insert infographic title], +[provides the data and information needed to illustrate the infographic] + [specifies the colors and fonts to be used in the infographic to be consistent with the theme and brand].*
Prompt 1	*"Act as an infographic designer and create one on "Artificial Intelligence in Education", use the Title "Learning in times of ChatGPT", use clear and concise text, stunning graphics and reliable fonts."*

| Prompt 2 | *"If I asked you to create an infographic on "Educational Innovation," how would you conceive it? I would want you to include a catchy title, explanatory text, representative graphics, and verifiable sources. Submit a proposal to me."* |

4. 5 GENERATING CREATIVE IDEAS FOR EDUCATIONAL GAMES

ChatGPT can assist in the development of educational games by providing creative ideas and suggestions on the elements that should be included in the game to make it effective and engaging for students. In addition, ChatGPT can provide information on the key concepts that should be addressed in the game and how they can be presented in a clear and understandable way. In summary, ChatGPT can be a useful tool for teachers to create educational games that are effective and engaging for their students. Here is an example of an application:

#40 Create educational games	
Objective	*Obtain ideas for the development of educational games as didactic support resources to complement the development of a subject of study.*
Template	*Generate some examples of educational games + that could be used in [course name] and give me [recommendations] to generate a [didactic resource] on the [subject] + they should be interactive.*
Prompt	*"Generate some examples of educational games that could be used in an Educational Technology course. Make sure the games are interactive and designed to help students better understand key educational technology concepts. It is also important that the games are fun and engaging for the students."*

4.6 SIMULATION BUILDING

ChatGPT can generate realistic scenarios that allow students to simulate real-life situations and practice skills and knowledge in a controlled environment. This type of resource is valuable for teachers who want to incorporate simulation-based learning into their courses.

#41 Create scenarios for simulations	
Objective	*Obtain ideas for the development of useful scenarios for the generation of educational simulations.*
Template	*Generate scenarios for simulations and give me [guidelines] to create a [type of resource] on [theme] + [associated didactic strategy].*
Prompt	*"Generate educational simulations and give me guidelines for creating teaching material on educational technology and project-based learning."*

4.7 CREATION OF VOCABULARY LISTS

A vocabulary list is a teaching resource that can be generated by the teacher to help students learn and remember specific terms related to a topic or discipline. This list can include keywords, definitions, and examples of usage in context. ChatGPT can support the implementation of a vocabulary list in two ways: (a) as a search tool; ChatGPT can help the teacher find keywords and precise definitions of a specific topic, which facilitates the creation of a complete and accurate vocabulary list, and (b) as an example generator; ChatGPT can provide in-context examples of word usage in a sentence or paragraph, which can help students better understand their meaning and application in practice. Here is an example application:

#42 Create vocabulary list	
Objective	*Generate proposals for the development of vocabulary lists as a support resource for the student.*
Template	*Create a vocabulary list that includes [guideline] with the topic [theme]. Be sure to provide [additional information or specific details] + [context].*
Prompt	*"Create a vocabulary list that includes at least 10 key terms related to the topic of emerging technologies in education. Be sure to provide a brief definition or explanation of each term so students can better understand its meaning."*

4. 8 CREATION OF FAQS

FAQs, or frequently asked questions, are useful learning material for students as they allow them to access important and relevant information quickly and easily. This type of material can answer common and frequently asked questions that may arise in relation to a specific topic, helping to save time and increase learning efficiency.

#43 Create Faqs	
Objective	*Generate Faqs proposals as a didactic resource for the student.*
Template	*Create a FAQ section for my [subject] course. Generate a list of questions and answers that may be useful to students.*
Prompt	*"Create a FAQ section for my course "Educational Technology". Generate a list of questions and answers that may be useful to students."*

4.9 CREATION OF STUDY GUIDES

Study guides are instructional materials that are intended to help students better organize and understand the content of a course. These guides may include questions, exercises and summaries that help students identify important topics, synthesize information and prepare for exams.

#44 Create Study Guides	
Objective	*Generate proposals for study guides as a didactic resource for students*
Template	*Create a study guide for the upcoming [subject] course exam in which you include a list of the [types of resources] .Reference the following agenda and learning objectives [reference]."*
Prompt	*"Create a study guide for the upcoming "Educational Technology" course exam in which you include a list of topics to be covered, review questions and practice exercises. Take this reference " "――" ".*

4.10 OTHER TYPE OF USES

A teacher can also use ChatGPT for writing a blog-type article, providing the main content to be covered and letting the language model generate the base text. The teacher can then edit and adjust the text to make sure it is clear and fits the learning objectives. In addition, the ChatGPT language model can provide additional suggestions and examples to include in the blog, which saves time and increases the quality of the content.

#45 Create blog articles	
Objective	*Generate proposals and content for blog articles*

Template	Write a blog article about [topic + features]. Be sure to address the following topics [questions related to the topic]. Be sure to provide [context].
Prompt	"Write a blog post in which you explain the importance of academic integrity in the context of virtual spaces. Be sure to address the following topics: ⁎ What is academic integrity and why is it important in the context of virtual spaces? ⁎ What are some of the ways students can violate academic integrity online? ⁎ What are some of the consequences of violating academic integrity? ⁎ How can students and faculty work together to ensure academic integrity in virtual spaces? Be sure to provide concrete examples and use reliable sources to support your arguments."

A teacher can also use ChatGPT to create a draft of a lecture to be delivered to students. This can be done by providing information on the topic to be covered in the presentation and then using the language model to generate ideas and suggestions on how to structure and organize the presentation. In addition, the model can help the teacher find and add relevant quotes and examples to support the key points of the presentation. In this way, the teacher can create an initial draft that can be edited and improved over time.

#46 Create conference structure proposals	
Objective	Generate proposals for the design and development of a conference structure.
Template	[context about what is being prepared] on [topic + characteristics]. Generate an initial conference proposal that includes [questions and/or examples related to the topic]. Give me [expected results related to the focus of the presentation].

Prompt	*"I am working on a proposal to present a conference on ChatGPT in higher education . Generate an initial conference proposal that includes the benefits of using natural language technology in learning, as well as some examples of success stories in implementing ChatGPT at different universities and educational programs. Give me some tips on how to approach the presentation effectively and how to present examples of use cases that are interesting and impactful to the attendees."*

ChatGPT can assist the teacher with the style and spelling review of study materials, such as study guides, slide presentations, and articles, among other things. By copying and pasting content into ChatGPT, the language model can analyze grammar, punctuation, spelling, and other aspects of writing style. ChatGPT can then provide suggestions for correcting grammatical and spelling errors, as well as improving the text's clarity and coherence. This can help the teacher create high-quality study materials that are easy for students to understand and read.

#47 Proofreading and spellchecking	
Objective	*Check spelling and style of a text or material to be delivered to students*
Template	*Review and correct the wording of the following text: [Copy here the text or reference to be reviewed].*
Prompt	*"Review and correct the wording of the following text: "A teacher can use ChatGPT for creating a draft for a lecture to be delivered to students by providing information about the topic to be addressed in the lecture and then using the language model to generate ideas and suggestions on how to structure and organize the presentation.""*

ChatGPT can help teachers rewrite content for different audiences through the generation of texts adapted to different levels of complexity, jargons and writing styles, which can be very useful for the creation of support materials for students.

#48 Rewriting content for different audiences	
Objective	*Targeting content to different audiences*
Template	*Rewrite the content of this material to make it more technical and appropriate for a specialized audience in the area. The text to be rewritten is as follows: [insert the text to be rewritten here].*
Prompt	*"Rewrite the content of this material to make it more technical and appropriate for a specialized audience in the area. The text to be rewritten is as follows: [insert the text to be rewritten here]"*

A teacher can use ChatGPT to generate summaries of articles or bibliographic references relevant to a specific topic. By using the ChatGPT language model, the teacher can enter the title of the article or bibliographic reference and obtain a concise summary that highlights the key points of the text. This can be especially useful for generating background material for students, as part of a bibliography, or to provide an overview of a particular topic. In addition, the teacher can also use it to generate automatic summaries of several articles or bibliographic references, which can save time and effort in researching and preparing supporting material for students. A basic instruction would be for example:

#49 Generation of summaries	
Objective	*Generate abstracts of articles, books, text or electronic reference.*
Template	*Create a summary of the following article [text, link, reference, etc.]. Give me an executive summary of [special features]+[additional information or specific details] + [context].*

Prompt	*"Create a summary of the following article "The Use of Technology in Distance Education". Give me a 300-word executive summary that includes the key points and major conclusions. I would like to include it in a presentation I will be making to my students in the next class."*

ChatGPT can support the teacher in language translation by generating accurate and contextual translations of whole texts or individual sentences. With its ability to understand the context and subtleties of language, ChatGPT can provide more accurate and consistent translations than traditional machine translators. This can be useful for teachers who work with students from different countries or who need access to resources in different languages to create support materials such as study guides, readings and other teaching materials.

#50 Language translation	
Objective	*Translate students' support material into any language.*
Template	*Translate the following material on the [topic]of [translation needs] so that my students can access the information in both languages. Generate an accurate and fluent translation that is easy to understand. Be sure to use [additional information or specific details] + [context].*
Prompt	*"Translate the following educational technology material from English to Spanish so that my students can access the information in both languages.Generate an accurate and fluent translation that is easy for non-Spanish speaking students to understand. Be sure to use appropriate academic language and avoid any literal translations that may confuse students."*

The use of images can significantly improve student understanding and learning. However, generating images to accompany educational material can be a costly and time-consuming process. In this context, the use of artificial intelligence (AI) tools such as DALL-E3, combined with the natural language of ChatGPT, presents itself as an efficient and effective solution for generating images from text. DALL-E3 is a high-quality image generation tool that uses a natural language model to interpret text input and produce a corresponding image. This tool is capable of producing detailed and realistic images, with the possibility of including complex objects and scenarios. In addition, DALL-E3 allows the generation of images in a wide range of styles and formats, making it suitable for a variety of educational applications.

The generation of images using DALL-E3 can improve the quality of educational material and provide students with a more enriching learning experience. In addition, this tool can be particularly useful for the creation of online learning materials and the production of distance learning resources. Using ChatGPT with DALL-E3 also allows for greater customization and adaptation of educational content to the specific needs of learners, which can further enhance the effectiveness of the teaching-learning process. By using DALL-E3 in conjunction with ChatGPT, visual content can be generated from text descriptions, such as landscapes, animals, objects, among others. To use DALL-E3 effectively, it is important to consider the following aspects:

* *The quality of the description: The description must be sufficiently detailed and specific so that DALL-E3 can generate a consistent and accurate image.*

* *The selection of styles and themes: DALL-E3 can generate images in a variety of styles and themes, so it is important to select the right style for the specific application.*

* *Image size and resolution: DALLE-3 can generate high-resolution images in a variety of sizes, so it is important to select the right size and resolution for the specific application.*

To experiment with the DALLE-3 tool, the first step is to access the tool's official website and register or log in via Google or Microsoft. Once you are logged in, you can start using the tool without difficulty. To start creating your first image, simply describe the image you want to generate in the central text box on the page. It is important to consider that the more detailed the description, the more accurate the image generated by the tool will be in relation to your preferences. For this purpose, ChatGPT can help you generate some basic instructions.

#51 Generate images from text	
Objective	Generate proposals for prompts to request the creation of images in DALL-E3
Template	Generates a photograph [Image overview], [General shot], [Shooting context], [Time and lighting details], [Type of lens used], [Focus effects] and [Type of device used for shooting].
Prompt	"Generates a vibrant photograph of a teacher, general shot, outdoors, golden hour sunset photo, wide angle lens, soft focus and taken with an iphone 12"

Bing, the well-known search engine developed by Microsoft, has emerged as a prominent alternative tool for the integration of DALL-E 3. This integration represents a significant milestone in the field of digital image synthesis and web search. Unlike the implementation of DALL-E 3 in environments such as ChatGPT, where the primary focus is on AI-assisted text generation, Bing offers a platform that combines web search with advanced image generation capabilities.

Importantly, Bing's adoption of DALL-E 3 differs from its use in ChatGPT in several key respects. While ChatGPT focuses on providing consistent and contextual textual responses, occasionally integrating image generation capabilities to complement these responses, Bing Create is more directly oriented toward generating images based on search and user queries. This allows Bing users to explore image generation in a more autonomous and targeted way, using the search engine to facilitate both information retrieval and visual content creation.

In addition, the integration of DALL-E 3 into Bing underscores the growing importance of intuitive user interfaces in accessing and using advanced AI technologies. By making AI image generation accessible through a familiar search engine, Bing lowers the barriers to entry for users who may not be familiar with more specialized platforms or AI techniques.

5. INNOVATING THE DESIGN OF LEARNING ACTIVITIES

Learning activities are fundamental to the educational process because they enable students to acquire knowledge, skills and competencies in an active and meaningful way. Rather than simply receiving information passively, learning activities engage students in the learning process, which can enhance their motivation, interest and understanding. Learning activities can foster skills such as collaboration, problem solving and creativity, which are critical in modern life and work. Here are some examples of applications.

5.1 CREATION OF DISCUSSION FORUMS

In the classroom, discussion is one of the most powerful teaching tools. In a face-to-face class or online class, you can use a discussion to encourage students' active participation in exploring and analyzing various topics and give them the opportunity to interact with and learn from their peers. The key to a good conversation is a well-crafted discussion question. A fundamental guideline could be, for instance:

#52 Create discussion and/or reflection forums	
Objective	Obtain ideas on how forums can be used to generate a space for discussion and/or reflection among students. Provide suggestions for composing forum instructions.
Template	Generate a discussion forum type activity, presenting [guidelines] on the [theme]. It is important that you consider [associated didactic strategy] + [context].
Prompt 1	"Generate a discussion forum type activity, posing two trigger questions on the topic "The role of technology in the continuous improvement of education". It is important that each student respond to at least one comment from his/her peers."
Prompt 2	"If we were organizing a forum on "Educational Innovation", what questions could be included so that participants could share their opinions and knowledge? Could you propose a structure for the forum that includes an introduction, several discussion questions, and a conclusion?"

A more specific instruction, where the creation of the instructions is requested, would be for example:

#53 Create instructions for a discussion and/or reflection forum	
Objective	Obtain instructions for the learning activity, written for students.

Template	Write the instructions for a discussion forum on [topic]. Include [guidelines and/or special features] + [context].
Prompt	"Write the instructions for a forum on the challenges of higher education. Include the following elements: a clear description of the topic, the objectives of the activity, the rules of participation, the question(s) to be answered, and the deadline for submission of the activity. Also, make sure the instructions are easy to follow and written in clear and precise language."

5. 2 CREATION OF COMPLETION EXERCISES

Quickly create fill-in-the-blank exercises with ChatGPT. This type of activity can be used to learn new content. A basic instruction would be for example:

#54 Create gap-filling exercises	
Objective	Obtain the design of the activity to complete spaces.
Template	Write a fill-in-the-blank exercise on the [topic] and create a fill-in-the-blank activity.
Prompt	"Write a paragraph on the topic "The role of the teacher in context of educational innovation" and create a fill-in-the-blank activity."

5. 3 CASE STUDY GENERATION

ChatGPT can be a valuable resource to help a teacher create a case study as a learning activity. By providing detailed information about a real situation or issue, case studies can help students understand theoretical concepts in a practical context. With ChatGPT, a teacher can request detailed information on a specific topic, such as educational innovation, and receive personalized suggestions for creating a comprehensive and engaging case study for students. A basic instruction would be for example:

#55 Create case studies	
Objective	Get some ideas of what kind of case studies you could use to develop a specific topic.
Template	Generate an [expected result], to evaluate [the criterion] + of a student on the [subject].
Prompt	"Generate a proposed case study to assess a student's understanding of the topic "Issues related to the use of technology in education"."

A more specific instruction would be for example:

#56 Create instructions for a specific case study	
Objective	Obtain instructions for the case study to be implemented
Template	I need a case study + on [subject] that can be used as teaching material for my students. Include [additional information or specific details] + [context].
Prompt 1	"I need a case study on "Educational Innovation" that can be used as teaching material for my students. Include a clear introduction to the topic, a detailed description of an innovative classroom initiative, and an analysis of its results and lessons learned. Present me with a concise and clear proposal. Write instructions for the student. Also, if possible, include some discussion questions so students can reflect on the lessons learned and apply them in their own context."
Prompt 2	"If I asked you to create a case study on "Educational Innovation," how would you conceive of it. Include a clear context, a problem to be solved, an innovative solution, and an analysis of results and lessons learned. Present me with a detailed proposal, instructions for the student, and how it might be evaluated."

5. 4 RESOURCES FOR PROJECT IDEAS

One of the advantages of using ChatGPT to find project ideas for learning assessment is that the model has access to a wide variety of knowledge and resources that can be useful in generating innovative and creative ideas. In addition, being an automated tool, it can generate multiple idea options in a short period of time, which saves time and effort for the teacher compared to manually searching for ideas. Another advantage is that ChatGPT can be tailored to the specific needs of the teacher, as it can customize ideas based on the learning objectives, available resources, and the time and budget constraints of the course. A basic instruction would be for example:

#57 Generate project ideas	
Objective	*Find ideas of types of projects that can be used to pursue a didactic objective.*
Template	*I need help to design a project on [subject] that can be used as teaching material for my students. Include [additional information or specific details] + [context].*
Prompt	*"I need help designing an educational technology project that can help my students improve their skills in assessment and feedback issues. I am looking for a solution that is accessible and appealing to graduate level students and can be implemented within 2 months on a limited budget. Can you provide me with some ideas that fit these requirements. Write the instructions for the student."*

5. 5 GENERATION OF SHORT STORIES

The use of storytelling in education is increasingly valued and appreciated. This technique consists of telling a story with a specific purpose, and can be used to achieve a wide variety of educational objectives. In education, storytelling is used to create a more friendly environment and to connect with students in a more personal and meaningful way. One of the main applications of storytelling in education is to promote understanding and retention of information. When a topic is presented through a story, it becomes easier for students to relate the content to their own lives and understand it in a deeper way. In addition, storytelling can also be used to teach social and emotional skills, such as empathy, communication and conflict resolution.

Another important application of storytelling in education is to motivate and inspire students. By telling stories related to the content being taught, it can illustrate how the knowledge and skills acquired in the classroom can be applied in real life and have a positive impact on the world. In addition, storytelling can also be used to help students develop their creativity and imagination. A basic instruction would be for example:

#58 Generate short stories (Storytelling)	
Objective	Obtain a short story (storytelling) to be used to present a specific topic.
Template	Generate a short story + on the [topic] that can be used as teaching material for my students. Include [additional information or specific details] + [context].
Prompt	"Generate a short story (Storytelling) around the theme "The role of technology in the continuous improvement of education", which promotes meaningful learning."

"SHORT STORYTELLING WITHIN EDUCATIONAL SETTINGS CAN SERVE AS A POWERFUL TOOL TO CAPTIVATE STUDENTS,

STIMULATE CREATIVITY AND CRITICAL THINKING, AND PROMOTE PROFOUND LEARNING EXPERIENCES."

This narrative approach can actively engage students by connecting them emotionally and intellectually with the content, making the learning process more relatable and memorable. By integrating short stories into the curriculum, educators can provide a dynamic platform for students to explore complex concepts and ideas in a more digestible and engaging manner. Moreover, short storytelling encourages students to think critically, as they analyze and interpret the narratives, fostering deeper understanding and retention of the material. It also provides a creative outlet for students to express their ideas and perspectives, enhancing their communication skills and boosting their confidence.

A more specific instruction, which includes the components of a story and highlights the approach to how the story should be told, would be for example:

#59 Generate short stories (Storytelling) Pro mode	
Objective	*Obtain a detailed short story (storytelling) that includes the plot and characters to be used to present a specific topic.*
Template	*Create a short story + on the [topic] that can be used as teaching material for my students. Include [additional information or specific details] + [context].*

Prompt	"Create an exciting and motivating story about how digital transformation is revolutionizing Universities. The story should emphasize the importance of keeping up with new technologies and how they can improve education. Include details that make it memorable and eye-catching.
	It should include plot, two main characters, and should be set in post-pandemic time. It should follow the following structure: Introduction: Introduces the characters, Development: The narrative contextualizes the setting and the characters show their characteristics in the story. Conflict: Here, the problem the main characters will face is introduced. Resolution: In this section we already solve the main conflict.Reflection: A very important aspect is to analyze what the students think about the story, the characters, the conflict and the solution."

5. 6 DIALOG GENERATION FOR DIGITAL SCENARIOS

Generating dialogues for digital scenarios is an essential tool to enhance the user experience and to provide more effective learning. Dialogues allow learners to interact with characters and situations that resemble reality, which improves knowledge retention and fosters critical thinking. In addition, creating realistic dialogues for digital environments can be challenging, as a balance between authenticity and simplicity is required. This is where ChatGPT can be a valuable tool. By utilizing its natural language generation capabilities, it can assist in the creation of realistic and effective dialogues for digital scenarios. By programming ChatGPT with certain parameters and specific details, you can generate dialogs that fit the user's needs, such as level of difficulty, tone, length, among others. This can save time and resources in creating content for virtual environments, and provide learners with a richer and more effective learning experience. A basic instruction would be for example:

#60 Create dialogues for digital scenarios	
Objective	*Create proposals for dialogues between two people*
Template	*Create a dialogue + on the [topic] that can be used as teaching material for my students. Include [additional information or specific details] + [context].*
Prompt	*"Create a dialogue between two people to depict and highlight "The role of technology in the continuous improvement of education." The dialogue will be used to develop a cartoon."*

A more specific instruction would be for example:

#61 Writing dialogs for digital scenarios in Pro mode	
Objective	*Write dialogues between two people in a professional manner.*
Template	*Write a dialogue + discussing [additional information] that can be used as teaching material for my students. Include [additional information or specific details] + [context].*
Prompt	*"Write a dialogue between two characters discussing the pros and cons of digital transformation in the university sector, include an introduction that establishes the characters and their relationship, and make the arguments clear and coherent. Name the characters and consider that the dialogues will be used to generate a podcast."*

5.7 TREASURE HUNT BUILDING

The treasure hunt is a playful and educational activity that engages students in exploring and discovering knowledge in a creative and exciting way. This learning technique can help students improve their ability to search for and synthesize information, as well as develop problem-solving and teamwork skills. ChatGPT can support you in developing this type of activity. A basic instruction would be for example:

#62 Generate Treasure Hunt	
Objective	*Generate proposals for the development of treasure hunt type learning activities.*
Template	*Describe an example of how a scavenger hunt type learning activity could be designed that could be used as teaching material for my students. Include [additional information or specific details] + [context].*
Prompt	*"Describe an example of how a "scavenger hunt" type learning activity could be designed to teach my students "the importance of feedback in their online learning process". The activity should include a series of challenges and puzzles that students have to solve to advance in their search for the perfect feedback. It should also include different resources, such as videos and articles, that show how constructive feedback can help improve academic and work performance. The activity should be designed to be completed within 1 week, individually and should be suitable for graduate students. Write instructions for the student and provide 5 bibliographic references or web page links for them to use in developing the activity."*

5. 8 WEBQUEST DESIGN

WebQuests are an educational tool that allows you to design online learning activities in a structured and guided way, focused on a specific topic of study. By designing a WebQuest, students can be provided with a clear and organized path to research and learn about a topic in an autonomous way, using resources selected and verified by the teacher. In this way, students are provided with an enriching and effective learning experience that allows them to reinforce the topic of study in a deeper and more meaningful way. A basic instruction would be for example:

#63 Webquest Generation	
Objective	*Generate proposals for the development of Webquest-type learning activities.*
Template	*Generate a Webquest + learning activity for my students in the [course name] + course to learn about [subject matter]. Write [expected result], it should take [additional information or specific details] + [context].*
Prompt	*"Generate a "Webquest" type learning activity for my students in the "Educational Innovation" course to learn about "the use of emerging educational technologies and their impact on education". Write the instructions for the activity, it should take into account the structure of a webquest and should be focused on graduate level students."*

5.9 ESCAPE ROOM DESIGN

Escape rooms, used as learning activities, are an innovative way to encourage student participation and active learning because they involve problem solving and teamwork. Immersion in a playful experience enables students to apply their knowledge in a more practical and creative manner, reinforcing the subject matter in a fun and memorable manner. In addition, escape rooms can also help develop communication, leadership, and critical thinking skills, which can be beneficial to their personal and professional development. Basic instruction would be, for example:

#64 Escape Room Generation	
Objective	*Generate proposals for the development of Escape Room type learning activities.*
Template	*[Didactic objective] + [course name] + on [subject matter]. Design an Escape room + type learning activity for my students in the [course name] + course to learn [didactic objective]. Write [expected result], you must take into account [additional information or specific details] + [context].*
Prompt	*"I am looking for an innovative way to teach my 'Educational Technology' students about the use of 'Gamification' in the classroom. I want students to experience first hand how this technology can be used in education, and how it can transform the way teaching and learning takes place. Design an 'Escape room' in which students have to solve a series of challenges and tests using 'Gamification' technology to advance in their quest. Design the structure of the game, the puzzles and provide some educational resources that you can use for the activity. Write the instructions for the student, the activity should be designed for graduate level students and can be completed in an estimated time of 1 hour."*

5. 10 GENERATING DIGITAL PORTFOLIOS

Digital portfolios are a valuable tool for students, as they allow them to collect and organize their work and projects electronically. Students can customize these portfolios to suit their needs and objectives, incorporating a variety of materials such as essays, presentations, and multimedia projects. By designing digital portfolios as learning activities, students can not only demonstrate what they have learned but they can also reflect on their learning process, identify strengths and weaknesses, and foster self-determination in their learning journey. Furthermore, the use of digital portfolios can help to develop technology skills, teamwork, and collaboration competencies by allowing for online interaction and feedback from peers and teachers. An example of basic instruction would be as follows:

#65 Generate digital portfolios	
Objective	*Generate proposals for the development of learning activities such as digital portfolios.*
Template	*Design a digital portfolio activity that allows + for my [course name] + course students to learn about [the topic]. Write [expected result], you must take [additional information or specific details] + [context]*
Prompt	*"Design a "digital portfolio" type activity that allows students in the "Educational Technology" course to reflect on their learning process and the use of technological tools. Write the instructions for the student."*

5. 11 BUILDING GROUP DYNAMICS

Group dynamics are important because they encourage collaborative learning and allow students to interact and share their knowledge. These activities not only enhance understanding of the subject matter, but also help develop social skills, such as effective communication, decision making and teamwork. In addition, group dynamics can make learning more interesting and fun, which can increase student motivation and engagement. A basic instruction would be for example:

#66 Generate group dynamics	
Objective	*Generate ideas for the development of group dynamics.*
Template	*Create a group dynamic that allows + for my students in the [course name] + course to learn about [subject matter] using [external resources] . [additional information or specific details] + [context] Provide [expected outcome] for students.*

Prompt	*"Create a group dynamic that allows students in the 'Educational Technology' course to work as a team to design an educational innovation project using technological tools. The activity should last approximately 1 hour and should encourage collaboration, creativity, and critical thinking. Provide detailed instructions for students."*

5. 12 GENERATING GROUP DISCUSSIONS

Group discussions are an important tool for encouraging students' active participation in the learning process. By participating in a debate, students are not only forced to analyze and understand different points of view, but also have the opportunity to express their own opinions and arguments. In addition, debates can help improve students' critical thinking skills and communication skills, which can be beneficial in both their academic life and future career. A basic instruction would be for example:

#67 Generate group discussions	
Objective	*Generate ideas for group discussion*
Template	*I want to promote [didactic objective] + on [thematic]. Give me a list of possible discussion topics related to [thematic] . Also, give me [additional information or specific details] + [context].*
Prompt	*"I want to encourage critical thinking and analysis of different perspectives on the impact of technology on education. Give me a list of possible discussion topics related to educational technology, along with possible arguments for each perspective. Also, give me a structure for leading the group discussion and some guidelines for evaluating student performance during the activity."*

5. 13 ROLE-PLAY STRATEGIES

Role-play activities are a valuable tool for learning as they allow students to experience real-life situations and practice skills and knowledge in a safe and controlled environment. In addition, they encourage critical thinking, empathy and creativity, which can help students better understand the topic of study and apply what they learn in real-life situations. A basic instruction would be for example:

#68 Generate role-play	
Objective	Generate ideas for the development of role-play type learning activities.
Template	Create a role-playing activity + that allows students in my course [subject] + [didactic objective]. The activity should [didactic objective]. Give me [additional information or specific details]+[context].
Prompt	"Create a 'role-play' activity that allows students in my 'Educational Technology' course to explore the different perspectives of stakeholders in the use of technology in the classroom, including teachers, students, parents, and administrators. The activity should encourage dialogue and reflection on the challenges and opportunities presented by the integration of technology in education. Give me some realistic scenarios and educational resources that I can use to guide discussion and critical analysis."

5. 14 GENERATING ACTIVITIES TO PROMOTE ACTIVE LEARNING

Learning activities that promote active learning and student participation are essential for students to reinforce a topic of study. Actively involving students in the learning process encourages critical reflection, practical application of knowledge, and the development of problem-solving skills. In addition, these activities promote long-term retention of information and enhance student motivation and engagement with the topic of study. A basic instruction would be for example:

#69 Generate active learning activities	
Objective	*Generate proposals for the development of active learning activities.*
Template	*Develop an activity that fosters active learning in the [subject matter] course, aimed at assisting students in achieving [educational objective]. It is recommended to incorporate [additional information or specific details] within the [context].*
Prompt	*Design an activity that encourages "active learning" in the "Educational Technology" course, which will assist students in applying the learned concepts and skills related to "Virtual and Augmented Reality". Suggest some resources and strategies that can be used to guide the activity.*

5. 15 GENERATING ACTIVITIES TO PROMOTE EXPERIENTIAL LEARNING

Experiential learning is an effective way to learn as it involves students in real and concrete situations, enabling them to apply knowledge and skills in a meaningful and practical context. By fostering experimentation and learning through experience, students can develop a deeper and more lasting understanding of the subject matter. Experiential learning can encourage critical thinking and problem-solving, and help students develop social and emotional skills. A basic instruction, for example, would be:

#70 Generate activity to promote experiential learning	
Objective	*Generate proposals for the development of experiential learning activities.*
Template	*Create an activity that promotes experiential learning in the [subject matter] course, designed to assist students in achieving [educational objective]. Instruct the students to [activity development]. It is recommended to include [additional information or specific details] within the [context].*
Prompt	*Create an activity that promotes experiential learning in the "Educational Technology" course, which helps students apply learned concepts and skills related to "Integrating Technology in Early Childhood Education". Instruct the students to become "technology mentors" for preschool or elementary children, and to develop an interactive teaching session on a technology-related topic, such as the use of educational apps or programming robots. The activity should include a planning, implementation, and evaluation process, and students should reflect on their experience as technology mentors. Suggest some resources and strategies that can assist students in planning and developing their teaching session.*

5.16 GENERATING ACTIVITIES TO PROMOTE THE "STEAM" APPROACH

The importance of creating activities that promote the STEAM approach (Science, Technology, Engineering, Arts, and Mathematics) lies in their ability to foster critical and creative thinking, and help students develop essential 21st-century skills such as problem-solving, collaboration, and communication.

By incorporating the STEAM approach into learning activities, students can apply theoretical concepts to real-world situations and learn in a more meaningful and relevant way. Furthermore, this approach can also motivate students to take an interest and engage with STEM subjects (Science, Technology, Engineering, and Mathematics), exploring how they can relate to the arts and creativity. A basic instruction, for example, would be:

#71 Generate learning activities with a STEAM focus	
Objective	Generate proposals for the development of STEAM-focused learning activities.
Template	Create a STEAM-focused learning activity that integrates technology and assists students in exploring the topic [subject matter]. Ensure that the activity involves [evaluation criteria]. Provide [additional information or specific details] within the [context].
Prompt	"Create a STEAM-focused learning activity that integrates technology and helps students explore the topic 'Types of Evaluation in the Teaching and Learning Process'. Ensure that the activity involves problem-solving, creativity, and critical thinking, as well as collaboration and communication in a team. Provide some resources and tools that can help students carry out the activity."

5.17 GENERATING FLIPPED CLASSROOM ACTIVITIES

The flipped classroom is a teaching methodology where students learn the basic concepts of a subject on their own time outside the classroom, and then use classroom time to apply, analyze, and deepen their understanding through practical and collaborative activities.

#72 Generate flipped classroom activities	
Objective	Generate proposals for the development of flipped classroom activities.

Template	Describe how you would apply the flipped classroom strategy to address the topic [subject matter]. [Questions related to the main features of the strategy]. Design a [expected outcome] + [additional information or specific details] + [context].
Prompt	"Describe how you would apply the flipped classroom strategy to address the topic 'educational technology'. What would be the content that students should review before the session? How would you structure the session itself to make the most of class time? How would you assess the students' understanding? Design a learning activity and write the instructions for the student."

5.18 INTEGRATION OF WEB 2.0 TOOLS

The integration of Web 2.0 tools in the development of learning activities refers to the use of various tools available on the web to enrich the teaching and learning process. ChatGPT can support educators in identifying useful Web 2.0 tools for their course, provide suggestions for integrating them effectively, and offer information on best usage practices. A basic instruction, for example, would be:

#73 Generate ideas for integrating Web 2.0 tools.	
Objective	Generate proposals for the integration of Web 2.0 tools in the development of learning activities.
Template	I would like to integrate Web 2.0 tools into my [subject matter] course to promote [educational objective]. Act as [role] and respond: [questions related to the integration process] + [additional information or specific details]. Draft [expected outcome].

Prompt	*"I would like to integrate Web 2.0 tools in my course to promote project-based learning. Act as an educational technology expert and respond: What tools do you recommend to enrich the learning process? How can I use these tools to develop activities that foster collaboration and active student participation? How can I structure the learning activities so that students use these tools effectively and collaborate with each other online? Draft an example of a learning activity where a Web 2.0 tool is used."*

6. DESIGN OF EVALUATIONS

ChatGPT can support the teacher in designing assessments by providing a variety of resources and suggestions. It can help generate questions and answers for tests and quizzes, provide sample rubrics for assessing projects and assignments, as well as offer guidance on how to effectively assess and provide feedback to students. In addition, ChatGPT can provide information and advice on different types of assessment, such as formative and summative assessment, and help teachers select the best option for their class and learning objectives. Overall, ChatGPT can provide valuable support for assessment design and help teachers improve the quality and effectiveness of their assessment practices.

6.1 GENERATING QUESTIONS

ChatGPT's ability to generate test questions based on a large amount of information allows teachers and instructors to create high-quality tests that accurately reflect students' knowledge of a given topic. In addition, ChatGPT can generate questions that can assess students' deep and meaningful knowledge, not just their short-term memory. A basic instruction would be for example:

#74 Generate multiple choice questions	
Objective	*Generate proposals of multiple choice questions for the development of an evaluation*
Template	*Give me a proposal of [number] multiple choice questions with their respective answers on the topic [thematic]*
Prompt	*"Give me a proposal of 3 multiple choice questions with their respective answers on the topic "Educational Innovation"."*

A more specific instruction making use of external resources could be for example:

#75 Generate multiple choice questions from a reference	
Objective	*Generate proposals of multiple choice questions for the development of an evaluation. Taking as reference external resources such as books, web pages, among others.*
Template	*Generate [number] multiple choice questions based on the article: [reference link or text or article name].*
Prompt	*"Genere 5 preguntas de opción múltiple basado en el artículo "coloque aquí su link de referencia".*

An instruction referencing a specific question type format would be for example:

#76 Generate true and false questions

Objective	Generate proposals of true and false questions for the development of an evaluation.
Template	Write [number] true/false questions based on the article: [reference link or text or name of article].
Prompt	"Write 3 "true-false" questions based on the article entitled "Seven Keys to Educational Innovation" written by "BERENICE PACHECO-SALAZAR"".

#77 Generate reading comprehension questions

Objective	Generate proposed reading comprehension questions for the development of an evaluation.
Template	Write [number] reading comprehension questions based on the following text: [reference text].
Prompt	"Write 3 "reading comprehension" questions, based on the following text: "Copy the text you want to use as a reference".

#78Generate practical problem type questions

Objective	Generate proposals of practical problem-type questions for the development of an evaluation.
Template	Write [number] practical problem-type questions to assess [learning objective] on the topic [subject].
Prompt	"Write 3 questions of type "practical problems to assess theoretical and applied knowledge" on the "topic of web 2.0 tools in education. "

#79 Generate matching type questions

Objective	Generate proposals of practical problem-type questions for the development of an evaluation.

Plantilla	*Using [thematic] as the topic, create [number] matching questions that assess [learning objective] on the topic [thematic]. Provide [additional information or specific details]+[context].*
Prompt	*"Using the TPACK model as your topic, create 2 matching questions that assess students' understanding of the different components of the model and how they relate to each other. Make sure the questions are clear and specific so students can answer them accurately."*

ChatGPT can support a teacher in developing a self-assessment test by providing different types of questions, including true/false, multiple choice, fill-in-the-blank and short essay, and by helping to create specific questions that assess a student's understanding of a particular topic. ChatGPT can also provide information about the topic to be assessed, such as definitions, examples, and case studies, which can help the teacher create more precise and focused questions. A basic instruction would be for example:

#80 Generate self-assessment tests	
Objective	*Generate proposals for self-assessment type examinations.*
Template	*Create a self-assessment test on [subject] + including at least [number, type of question]. Questions should assess [learning objective]. Provide [additional information or specific details]+[context].*
Prompt	*"Create a self-assessment exam on the topic of academic integrity that includes at least 10 questions of different types, such as true/false, multiple choice, fill-in-the-blank, and short essay. The questions should assess the student's understanding of the importance of academic integrity, the different forms of plagiarism and how to prevent it, the consequences of lack of academic integrity, and how to properly cite sources. Make sure the questions are clear, precise, and focused on the key concepts of the topic."*

6.2 EVALUATION TOOLS

Assessment instruments are tools used to measure students' performance, knowledge or skills in a given area. The main purpose of assessment instruments is to provide information about the level of student learning in a specific subject area, which allows teachers to adjust their teaching to help students achieve their educational goals. They are also used to make informed decisions about student grading and provide feedback to improve student learning. Assessment rubrics are tools that establish criteria and performance standards for evaluating student performance on a specific task. ChatGPT can assist teachers in the design and development of assessment rubrics in a variety of ways.

#81 Create evaluation rubrics	
Objective	*Create evaluation rubric proposals.*
Template	*Create an evaluation rubric for an activity type [type of activity] + which will be included in the course [subject]. The student must [share the evaluation criteria]. The rubric should reference the [learning objective] and provide a detailed description of each level of performance for each criterion. Provide [additional information or specific details]+[context].*
Prompt 1	*"Create an evaluation rubric for a "Digital Portfolio" type learning activity which will be included in the "Educational Innovation" course. The student must design, build and publish resources. The rubric should include clear evaluation criteria related to the use of web 2.0 tools, graphic design, content presentation and activity design and provide a detailed description of each level of performance for each criterion. Weighting should be provided for each assessment criterion."*

Prompt 2	*"If I asked you to create a rubric to assess knowledge about types of evaluation in education, how would you conceive it? Include clear and objective criteria, as well as a grading scale and a detailed description of each performance level. Present me with a detailed proposal."*
Prompt 3	*"Create an evaluation rubric for an educational innovation project that includes criteria for creativity, originality, feasibility, and relevance. Provide a detailed description of each performance level for each criterion."*

#82 Generate Pro Mode Evaluation Rubrics.	
Objective	*Generate proposals for detailed evaluation rubrics.*
Template	*Generate an evaluation rubric in [delivery format] to assess student performance in presenting a [type of activity] in the [subject matter] course. Be sure to include the following fields: [fields of the table].*
Prompt	*"Generate an evaluation rubric in table format to assess student performance in presenting a final project in the 'Educational Innovation' course. Ensure to include the following fields: evaluation criteria, performance levels, description of each level, percentage weight of each criterion, and space for additional comments."*

Checklists are simpler assessment tools used to verify whether certain tasks or specific skills have been accomplished. Unlike a rubric, the checklist assesses the presence or absence of some behavior, skill, knowledge, ability, or attitude. The response will always be yes or no.

#83 Provide checklist	
Objective	*Generate proposals for detailed checklist.*
Template	*Create a checklist in [delivery format] to assess the [type of activity] of students in the [subject matter] course. Ensure that the checklist includes [evaluation criteria]. Provide [additional information or specific details] + [context].*

Prompt	*"Create a checklist in table format to evaluate the digital portfolio of students in the educational innovation course. Ensure that the checklist includes criteria to assess the organization of the portfolio, clarity of objectives, quality of content, and overall presentation of the portfolio. Provide a brief description of each criterion and a space for providing detailed and constructive feedback to the students."*

6. 3 EFFECTIVE FEEDBACK

Feedback is an essential part of the teaching-learning process, as it allows students to identify what skills or knowledge they need to improve and enables teachers to adjust their teaching to meet the individual needs of students. Effective feedback provides specific, objective, and useful information for students, helping them develop self-regulation and critical thinking skills. One way to use ChatGPT in feedback processes could be by creating a useful format to provide feedback on an activity. A basic instruction, for example, would be:

#84 Create format to provide effective feedback	
Objective	*Generate proposals for formats to provide effective feedback.*
Template	*Create a format for providing feedback to students on their participation in a [type of activity]. Provide [additional information or specific details] + [context]*
Prompt	*"Create a format for providing feedback to students on their participation in a group problem-solving activity. Be sure to include fields to identify strengths and areas for improvement in student performance, as well as specific suggestions for improving their work in future similar activities."*

The "Daniel Wilson Feedback Ladder" is a framework that describes the different levels of feedback that can be provided to students to help them improve their work. It begins with descriptive comments about what is right or wrong, and progresses towards identifying opportunities for improvement and specific suggestions on how to address them. ChatGPT can be useful for generating the Daniel Wilson Feedback Ladder by providing specific suggestions on the type of comments that can be offered at each level of the ladder, and also offering examples of how to do it. A basic instruction, for example, would be:

#85 Providing Wilson's feedback ladder	
Objective	Generate proposals for Daniel Wilson's feedback ladders to provide effective feedback to students.
Template	Create a feedback guide for students based on the "Daniel Wilson Feedback Ladder". Be sure to provide [additional information or specific details] + [context].
Prompt	"Create a feedback guide for students based on the 'Daniel Wilson Feedback Ladder' that they can use to revise and improve their own work in the final project of the educational innovation course. Be sure to provide specific examples of the types of feedback they should look for at each level of the feedback ladder to improve their work and earn a higher grade."

Use ChatGPT to provide personalized feedback on each student's performance. ChatGPT can analyze students' responses to specific questions and provide individualized real-time feedback on their performance. For example, the teacher can ask ChatGPT to provide specific feedback on the positive and negative aspects of each response and suggest areas of improvement for the student. A basic instruction, for example, would be:

#86 Provide personalized feedback	
Objective	Generate feedback proposals based on each of the response.

Template	*In my course [subject] + [context] I defined the following activity + [copy here the instruction of the learning activity], based on the above, provide personalized feedback to my student [student's name] who responded in this way in the forum [place here the answer given by the student] + provide feedback of type [type of feedback].*
Prompt	*"In my "Educational Innovation" course, I defined the following activity in a discussion forum "Provide 2 examples of emerging technologies in education", based on the above, provide the personalized feedback to my student "Juan Morales" who responded this way in the forum "The two main emerging technologies in education are artificial intelligence and STEAM. Provide constructive feedback".*

Use ChatGPT to personalize learning guidance and recommendations: ChatGPT can analyze each student's learning data and suggest personalized guidance to improve their understanding and performance. For example, the teacher can ask ChatGPT to provide individualized learning recommendations based on each student's strengths and weaknesses, and to offer suggestions for additional resources that can help improve their learning. A basic instruction would be for example:

#87 Provide structured feedback	
Objective	*Generate structured feedback proposals for students, with the objective of highlighting aspects that need to be improved.*
Template	*Create a set of questions that students can use to reflect on their performance on the topic [assessed topic] according to the results of the evaluation criteria and identified improvements: [results of the evaluation rubric].*

Prompt 1	*"Create a set of questions that students can use to reflect on their performance on the topic "Storytelling in Education" according to the results to the assessment criteria and identified improvements: Narrative quality: 7/10 Coherence: 8/10 Originality: 6/10".*
Prompt 2	*"Generate a series of specific steps to be followed by a student who has submitted the essay/paper described above, so that they can improve their performance in: Content: 8/10 Structure: 6/10 Coherence and cohesion: 7/10 Spelling and grammar: 9/10".*

Use ChatGPT to create and send personalized follow-up messages: ChatGPT can help teachers stay in touch with students and provide them with individualized guidance. For example, the teacher can ask ChatGPT to send follow-up messages to students, review their progress, and provide guidance and motivation to continue learning.

#88 Generate feedback messages (email and/or notices)	
Objective	*Generate proposals for feedback messages that can be sent through the means of communication defined in the platform, such as email.*
Template	*Write a feedback message to [student's name] about the submitted activity [insert the text submitted by the student]. Focus on highlighting a strength of the student's work and suggest a specific strategy for the student to improve in one of the areas of weakness in the assignment. Be sure to be specific and offer concrete suggestions. The message should be written [additional information or specific details] + [context].*

Prompt	*"Write a feedback message to Juan Perez about the activity performed (place the text of the assignment submitted). Focus on highlighting a strength of the student's work and suggest a specific strategy for him to improve in one of the areas of weakness in his assignment. Be sure to be specific and offer concrete suggestions. The message should be written as an e-mail format and should be motivational."*

Creating progress reports is a continuous evaluation process that allows the teacher to collect and analyze information about the students' performance in the course, in order to identify strengths and weaknesses and make adjustments in teaching to improve learning.

These reports usually include information on academic performance, class participation, attendance, among other relevant aspects. A basic instruction would be for example:

#89 Create progress reports	
Objective	*Generate proposals for the structure and types of progress reports that can be generated to provide overall feedback.*
Template	*Create a progress report on the activity [activity name + characteristics]. Analyzes [evaluation criterion] expressed in their contributions in the forum by the students, and evaluates their [evaluation criterion]. Includes [additional information or specific details] + [context].*
Prompt	*"Create a progress report on the activity "application of technological tools in the classroom". Analyzes the "level of adoption and use of these tools" expressed in their contributions in the forum by students, and evaluates their impact on the teaching and learning process. It includes recommendations for improving their use and exploitation".*

ChatGPT can support the teacher in analyzing student data from a course by processing natural language and generating reports and analysis based on the available data. For example, it can help identify patterns and trends in student data such as grades, performance on tests and assessments, and participation in online discussions.

#90 Analyze data	
Objective	*Analyze student data*
Template	*Generate a report showing the distribution of [data for analysis]. Identify any patterns or trends in the grades and + [additional information or specific details] + [context].*
Prompt	*"Generate a report showing the distribution of grades in the last exam and the number of students who earned each grade. Identify any patterns or trends in the grades and suggests possible factors that might have affected student performance."*

7. RESEARCH

Generative artificial intelligence, with its remarkable capacity to process, analyze, and synthesize vast amounts of data, brings a fresh perspective to the table. It challenges established notions and opens new avenues in research methodologies. Imagine the immense value of engaging in a brainstorming session with some of the most brilliant minds throughout history. This scenario, or the chance to delve into concepts from diverse perspectives – including those beyond your field of expertise – is now more accessible. ChatGPT emulates this enriching experience, offering a broad spectrum of ideas and viewpoints that can profoundly augment your research. This tool goes beyond simply generating novel ideas; it actively prompts the exploration of possibilities that may have been previously disregarded or unconsidered. ChatGPT can be an ally in different phases of research and is useful for:

* Generating innovative and under explored research topics and ideas.
* Advising and validating these topics, providing an objective, data-based perspective.
* Analyzing the subject of study from multiple approaches, enriching the understanding of the topic.
* Developing specific, results-oriented research questions: Using ChatGPT to generate research questions can serve as a starting point for deeper exploration.
* Inspiring researchers to consider perspectives or angles they had not previously contemplated. The depth and quality of subsequent analysis and research, however, will depend on the rigor and expertise of the researcher.
* Summarizing key information, thus facilitating access to essential knowledge in less time.
* Formulating hypotheses and clear objectives, outlining paths for effective investigations.
* Discovering and applying new research models, adapting to current needs.
* Finding relevant and up-to-date data and statistics.
* Devising creative headlines and approaches for articles and papers.
* Analyzing large amounts of data.

A researcher can use ChatGPT as a powerful tool, but it should complement and enrich the research process, not replace it. The researcher's knowledge, experience, and critical judgment remain irreplaceable in the pursuit of knowledge and the conduct of rigorous scientific research. Below, I share with you a series of effective prompts that are useful for different scientific research processes.

7.1 GENERATE RESEARCH TOPICS AND IDEAS

This type of prompt seeks to generate a series of research topics and ideas. We expect ChatGPT to propose novel and relevant proposals, each justifying its importance and potential impact on the specific field of study.

This approach aims to identify key areas for future research, thereby contributing to the advancement and enrichment of knowledge in the relevant discipline.

#91 Generate research topics and ideas	
Objective	Generate proposals for innovative research topics that address the current and future challenges of using specific technologies or methods in specific contexts.
Template	Act as a scientific researcher with over [X] years of experience in the field of [specific field]. Based on your extensive knowledge and considering the current and future challenges of using [specific technology or method] in [specific context], suggest [number] innovative research topics. These topics should address both the opportunities and challenges that [specific technology or method] presents in [specific context]. Include a brief description of why each topic is relevant and what specific problems it could help to solve or explore. Present your suggestions in the form of a bullet list, ensuring that each idea reflects a deep understanding of current trends and future needs in the field of [specific field].

Prompt	*"Act as a scientific researcher with over 10 years of experience in the field of educational technology and artificial intelligence. Based on your extensive knowledge and considering the current and future challenges of using AI in higher education, suggest 5 innovative research topics. These topics should address both the opportunities and challenges that AI presents in educational contexts. Include a brief description of why each topic is relevant and what specific problems it could help to solve or explore. Present your suggestions in the form of a bullet list, ensuring that each idea reflects a deep understanding of current trends and future needs in the field of higher education."*

7.2 ADVISING AND VALIDATING RESEARCH TOPICS AND IDEAS

This type of prompts is intended to advise and validate research topics and ideas. The intention is to use ChatGPT to review and evaluate research proposals, providing critical and constructive feedback. This includes analyzing the relevance, feasibility and originality of each proposed topic, as well as suggesting possible improvements or alternative approaches. The aim is to strengthen the quality and relevance of research, ensuring that it is aligned with academic standards and current trends in the corresponding field of study.

#92	
Objective	*Evaluate and provide feedback on potential research topics, focusing on their relevance, feasibility, and potential impact in the specified field, and suggest effective methodologies or approaches for investigation.*

Template	As an expert in [educational innovation and artificial intelligence], evaluate and provide feedback on the following list of potential research topics that I have developed. These topics focus on [the impact of AI on education]. For each topic, provide a critical analysis of its current relevance, feasibility, and potential impact on the field. In addition, suggest possible methodologies or approaches that could be effective in investigating these topics. Here is the list of topics: [list of topics].
Prompt	"As an expert in educational innovation and artificial intelligence, evaluate and provide feedback on the following list of potential research topics that I have developed. These topics focus on the impact of AI on education. For each topic, provide a critical analysis of its current relevance, feasibility, and potential impact on the field. In addition, suggest possible methodologies or approaches that could be effective in investigating these topics. Here is the list of topics: Ethical Analysis of AI in Education, adaptation of evaluation processes, regulation, risks."

7. 3 ANALYZE THE OBJECT OF STUDY FROM MULTIPLE PERSPECTIVES

ChatGPT is intended to examine a specific research topic from different angles, considering a variety of theoretical, methodological and practical approaches. This involves exploring different dimensions and possible interpretations of the topic, identifying how each perspective provides a richer and more nuanced understanding. The goal is to offer a comprehensive and diversified analysis, reflecting the complexity of the object of study and providing a solid foundation for deeper and more holistic research.

#93	
Objective	*Analyze the impact of AI on education from diverse perspectives, providing a comprehensive overview of its effects on various aspects of education.*
Template	*Act as an expert in [Artificial Intelligence and educational innovation]. Analyze the impact of AI on education from diverse perspectives, including [pedagogical, technological, ethical, social, and economic]. For each perspective, briefly describe how AI affects or could affect that aspect of education. Present your analysis in a bulleted list, making sure to cover a variety of viewpoints and types of interest.*
Prompt	*"Act as an expert in Artificial Intelligence and educational innovation. Analyze the impact of AI on education from diverse perspectives, including pedagogical, technological, ethical, social, and economic. For each perspective, briefly describe how AI affects or could affect that aspect of education. Present your analysis in a bulleted list, making sure to cover a variety of viewpoints and types of interest."*

7.4 FORMULATE RESEARCH QUESTIONS

ChatGPT is intended to generate specific and pertinent questions that guide the exploration of a given topic of study. These questions should be designed to prompt in-depth and critical inquiry, focusing on areas that require clarification, exploration, or more detailed analysis. The intent is to establish a clear and focused research framework that will help define the scope, objectives, and direction of future research in the selected field of study.

Objective	Formulate key research questions to investigate how AI can transform education, addressing various aspects such as personalization, student achievement and engagement, ethical considerations, and the role of educators.
Template	Act as an [educational technology specialist] with a focus on the application of [Artificial Intelligence in teaching and learning]. I need to formulate key research questions for a study investigating how AI can transform education. These questions should explore the effectiveness of AI in [personalizing learning], its impact on [student achievement and engagement], and [ethical considerations] related to [privacy and data bias]. In addition, include questions that assess the effect of AI on the [role and function of educators]. Provide a list of detailed and relevant questions that address these issues.
Prompt	"Act as an educational technology specialist with a focus on the application of Artificial Intelligence in teaching and learning. I need to formulate key research questions for a study investigating how AI can transform education. These questions should explore the effectiveness of AI in personalizing learning, its impact on student achievement and engagement, and ethical considerations related to privacy and data bias. In addition, include questions that assess the effect of AI on the role and function of educators. Provide a list of detailed and relevant questions that address these issues."

7. 5 SUMMARIZE RELEVANT INFORMATION (DATA SHEETS)

ChatGPT is intended to condense and synthesize key data on a specific topic, extracting the most important aspects and presenting them in a clear and concise manner. The goal is to produce informative summaries that provide a quick and accurate overview of the object of study, including essential details such as characteristics, findings, theories, and relevant conclusions. These summaries are intended to facilitate understanding and quick access to critical information, serving as an efficient tool for reference and analysis in subsequent research or studies.

#95	
Objective	*Create clear, concise summaries of complex texts, highlighting the most important concepts and presenting key points in a digestible format.*
Template	*Imagine you are a scientist with extensive experience in [information synthesis]. Your skill is to create clear, concise summaries free of complex jargon. Please summarize the following text, focusing on extrapolating and highlighting its most important concepts. Start with a concise paragraph of no more than [100 words]. Then, present the key points in a bulleted list format. Conclude with a one-sentence summary that captures the essence of the text. The text I need to summarize is: [Insert text here].*
Prompt	*"Imagine you are a scientist with extensive experience in information synthesis. Your skill is to create clear, concise summaries free of complex jargon. Please summarize the following text, focusing on extrapolating and highlighting its most important concepts. Start with a concise paragraph of no more than 100 words. Then, present the key points in a bulleted list format. Conclude with a one-sentence summary that captures the essence of the text. The text I need to summarize is: [Insert text here]."*

7. 6 DEVELOPMENT OF HYPOTHESES AND OBJECTIVES

ChatGPT is expected to assist in formulating clear and well-supported hypotheses, as well as defining specific and achievable objectives. This task involves identifying and articulating logical assumptions or predictions based on existing knowledge, and establishing clear goals to guide the research process. The focus is on creating a solid foundation for research, ensuring that both hypotheses and objectives are relevant, specific, and consistent with the chosen topic of study.

#96	
Objective	*Formulate specific hypotheses and define research objectives to investigate the impact of AI on the personalization of learning in online educational environments, considering aspects such as learning effectiveness, learner engagement, and ethical implications.*
Template	*As a researcher specializing in the convergence of [Artificial Intelligence and education], I am exploring how AI can enhance the personalization of learning in [online educational environments]. Based on current trends and existing research, formulate a specific hypothesis that examines the impact of AI on [learning personalization]. In addition, define [three] research objectives that will allow me to comprehensively investigate this hypothesis, considering aspects such as [learning effectiveness, learner engagement, and ethical implications of AI in education].*
Prompt	*"As a researcher specializing in the convergence of Artificial Intelligence and education, I am exploring how AI can enhance the personalization of learning in online educational environments. Based on current trends and existing research, formulate a specific hypothesis that examines the impact of AI on learning personalization. In addition, define three research objectives that will allow me to comprehensively investigate this hypothesis, considering aspects such as learning effectiveness, learner engagement, and ethical implications of AI in education."*

7.7 DISCOVER AND USE NEW RESEARCH MODELS

ChatGPT is intended to identify and suggest innovative approaches and emerging methodologies in the field of research. The intention is to explore and apply models that may offer new perspectives, overcome limitations of traditional approaches, or improve the efficiency and effectiveness of the research process. This approach focuses on keeping abreast of the latest trends and advances in the field of study, constantly seeking ways to innovate and enrich research practices.

#97	
Objective	*Identify and suggest innovative approaches and emerging methodologies in the field of research. The intention is to explore and apply models that may offer new perspectives, overcome limitations of traditional approaches, or improve the efficiency and effectiveness of the research process. This approach focuses on keeping abreast of the latest trends and advances in the field of study, constantly seeking ways to innovate and enrich research practices.*
Template	*Act as a scientific researcher with over [X] years of experience in the field of [educational technology and artificial intelligence]. Based on your extensive knowledge and considering the current and future challenges of using [AI in higher education], suggest [number] innovative research topics. These topics should address both the opportunities and challenges that [AI presents in educational contexts]. Include a brief description of why each topic is relevant and what specific problems it could help to solve or explore. Present your suggestions in the form of a bullet list, ensuring that each idea reflects a deep understanding of current trends and future needs in the field of [higher education].*

Prompt	*"Act as a scientific researcher with over 10 years of experience in the field of educational technology and artificial intelligence. Based on your extensive knowledge and considering the current and future challenges of using AI in higher education, suggest 5 innovative research topics. These topics should address both the opportunities and challenges that AI presents in educational contexts. Include a brief description of why each topic is relevant and what specific problems it could help to solve or explore. Present your suggestions in the form of a bullet list, ensuring that each idea reflects a deep understanding of current trends and future needs in the field of higher education."*

7. 8 DISCOVER INTERESTING FACTS AND STATISTICS

The objective is to discover interesting data and statistics that can enrich an area of study or research. ChatGPT is intended to identify and extract relevant quantitative information, providing insights and key findings. This includes finding and analyzing trends, patterns and correlations in datasets, in order to provide a deeper, evidence-based understanding of the topic in question. The goal is to offer a valuable resource to support arguments, formulate hypotheses or simply to provide an enriching quantitative perspective on the object of study.

#98	
Objective	*Discover interesting data and statistics that can enrich an area of study or research by identifying and extracting relevant quantitative information. Provide insights and key findings, analyzing trends, patterns, and correlations in datasets to offer a deeper, evidence-based understanding of the topic. The goal is to support arguments, formulate hypotheses, or provide an enriching quantitative perspective on the object of study.*

Template	As an expert researcher in [behavioral psychology], you possess a unique ability to identify under-explored areas of research. I need you to suggest [five] innovative studies that could be conducted to uncover new data and perspectives on [the impact of technology on mental health]. For each suggested study, provide a brief description of the research approach, the methods that could be used, and the type of data or results we hope to obtain. Ensure the studies aim to discover interesting facts and statistics that can enrich our understanding of this area.
Prompt	"As an expert researcher in behavioral psychology, you possess a unique ability to identify under-explored areas of research. I need you to suggest five innovative studies that could be conducted to uncover new data and perspectives on the impact of technology on mental health. For each suggested study, provide a brief description of the research approach, the methods that could be used, and the type of data or results we hope to obtain. Ensure the studies aim to discover interesting facts and statistics that can enrich our understanding of this area."

7.9 GET INTERESTING IDEAS FOR HEADLINES AND ARTICLES

The goal is to get interesting ideas for headlines and articles. ChatGPT seeks to generate creative and engaging suggestions for writing topics, focusing on capturing the reader's attention and addressing relevant aspects of the field of study. The intention is to inspire article titles and approaches that are both informative and engaging, providing a basis for content that not only informs but also engages and stimulates the audience.

Objective	Generate compelling titles for papers that reflect innovative research and key findings, capturing attention in academic publications and conferences. The goal is to present research findings in an impactful way, ensuring they align with current trends and topics of interest in the field.
Template	As an expert in [cognitive neuroscience], I have a number of research findings that I need to present in an impactful way. Based on current trends and topics of interest in [cognitive neuroscience], suggest [five] compelling titles for papers that reflect innovative research and key findings in this field. For each proposed title, include a brief explanation of how it encapsulates the essence and importance of the study, and how it could capture attention in academic publications and conferences.
Prompt	"As an expert in cognitive neuroscience, I have a number of research findings that I need to present in an impactful way. Based on current trends and topics of interest in cognitive neuroscience, suggest five compelling titles for papers that reflect innovative research and key findings in this field. For each proposed title, include a brief explanation of how it encapsulates the essence and importance of the study, and how it could capture attention in academic publications and conferences."

7.10 IMPROVING STYLE AND PROOFREADING IN ACADEMIC ARTICLES

ChatGPT also possesses the capability to assist in style improvement and linguistic proofreading. When crafting academic papers, the clarity and accuracy of idea communication are paramount. ChatGPT can aid in suggesting reformulations to enhance text coherence and fluency, in addition to correcting grammatical and syntactical errors. This ensures that the content is not only scientifically robust but also accessible and readable. Moreover, language translation plays a pivotal role in disseminating research to a global audience. ChatGPT enables the translation of academic papers while preserving fidelity to the original content and technical precision. This feature is especially valuable for researchers aiming to publish in international journals or collaborate with colleagues from different countries.

#100	
Objective	Enhance the quality and clarity of academic manuscripts by proofreading for spelling and grammatical errors, improving the articulation of ideas, and ensuring clarity in the presentation of complex concepts. Focus on the fluency of the narrative and the explanation of practical applications and research data interpretation in a formal, scientific language.
Template	As the author of a study on the implementation of [Artificial Intelligence in education], I seek to improve the quality and clarity of my manuscript. Proofread my text, identify and correct spelling and grammatical errors. In addition, provide recommendations for improving the articulation of ideas, clarity in the presentation of complex concepts, and fluency in the narrative. Pay particular attention to how practical applications of [AI in educational settings] and interpretation of research data are explained. It should be written in formal, scientific language. Highlight the aspects that I should adjust. Text to be reviewed: [Place here the text to be reviewed].

Prompt	"As the author of a study on the implementation of Artificial Intelligence in education, I seek to improve the quality and clarity of my manuscript. Proofread my text, identify and correct spelling and grammatical errors. In addition, provide recommendations for improving the articulation of ideas, clarity in the presentation of complex concepts, and fluency in the narrative. Pay particular attention to how practical applications of AI in educational settings and interpretation of research data are explained. It should be written in formal, scientific language. Highlight the aspects that I should adjust. Text to be reviewed: [Place here the text to be reviewed]."
Prompt 2	"Act as an expert in proofreading and editing academic texts in the field of [specific topic, e.g., 'environmental science' or 'cultural studies']. I have a manuscript on [specific article topic, such as 'wetland conservation' or 'the influence of film on contemporary culture'] that needs to be fine-tuned for style and clarity. Please proofread the text thoroughly, correcting spelling and grammatical errors. Eliminate filler words and unnecessary jargon to ensure that the language is clear and direct. Also, vary the length of sentences to keep the text interesting and engaging. Avoid the use of bullet points and present corrections and suggestions in easy-to-read paragraphs." Text to Review"" .
Prompt 3	"Act as a translator specializing in academic documents. I need to translate an article [specify source language, e.g. 'from Spanish to English'] on [specific topic, such as 'molecular biology of rare diseases']. The document contains technical terminology and complex concepts. Please be sure to maintain technical accuracy and academic tone in the translation. Also, be aware of cultural and linguistic differences that may affect the interpretation of certain terms. Provide a translation that is faithful to the original but also clear and understandable to an international audience."

8. CONCLUSIONS

Throughout this book, we have seen the importance of writing clear and concise prompts to converse with ChatGPT. This is critical to achieving meaningful and successful interactions. By providing specific and precise instructions, you can steer Chat GPT in the desired direction and ensure that the outcome is relevant and useful.

A clear and concise prompt is essential for ChatGPT to understand exactly what is being requested. If the prompt is vague or poorly defined, the result may be irrelevant or difficult to understand. On the other hand, a well-defined prompt allows Chat GPT to provide accurate and useful information, which can be beneficial in many areas, including data analysis.

In education, this can be particularly useful for providing guidance and support to students, as well as for developing more effective and personalized educational resources.

To improve your skills in creating effective ChatGPT prompts, it is important to practice and experiment with different approaches and styles. You can also solicit constructive feedback from friends and colleagues, as well as learn from the experiences of other successful users. Maintaining current knowledge of artificial intelligence and ChatGPT is crucial to using the best prompt delivery methods. In summary, improving your ability to define ChatGPT messages effectively through practice and collaboration is a valuable skill. So, don't hesitate to keep practicing and experimenting to hone your skills. In conclusion, the potential of ChatGPT in an educational setting is vast and exciting. As we have seen throughout this book, the use of clear and accurate prompts can help improve communication and understanding between humans and machines, which can have a positive impact on teaching and learning. Have you found this book helpful? Share it with your colleagues so they can benefit from ChatGPT. Together, we can advance the use of technology to improve education and learning.

REFERENCES

- ChatGPT (OpenAI, [2023]) - https://openai.com/
- What Is Chat GPT? - 10 Ways to USE Chat GPT for Students https://collegevidya.com/blog/how-to-use-chat-gpt-for-students
- 5 Ways for Teachers to Use ChatGPT https://www.thedaringenglishteacher.com/2023/01/5-ways-for-teachers-to-use-chatgpt.html
- 100 Best ChatGPT Prompts to Unleash AI's Potential https://mpost.io/100-best-chatgpt-prompts-to-unleash-ais-potential/
- ChatGPT: How to write the perfect prompts https://neuroflash.com/chatgpt-how-to-write-the-perfect-prompts/
- 120 Best CHAT GPT Prompts To Use Chat GPT Like a Ninja https://www.greataiprompts.com/chat-gpt/best-chat-gpt-prompts/
- The Ultimate ChatGPT Guide https://tested-salto-cab.notion.site/The-Ultimate-ChatGPT-Guide-8800517adc0d4c569d4a317c177185a1
- 250+ Most Useful ChatGPT Prompts Examples To Unleash The Power of AI https://www.learnprompt.org/chatgpt-prompts-examples/
- 140+ Act As Chat GPT Prompts to Transform It into Your Personal Advisor https://www.learnprompt.org/act-as-chat-gpt-prompts/
- ChatGPT Prompts for Teachers: Unlocking the Potential of AI in Education https://www.learnprompt.org/chat-gpt-prompts-for-teachers/
- Learn Prompting A Free, Open Source Course on Communicating with Artificial Intelligence https://learnprompting.org/es/
- Teachers, Meet ChatGPT: Your Very Own Personal Assistant https://www.suraasa.com/blog/chatgpt-for-teachers
- The ChatGPT Cheat Sheet https://www.kdnuggets.com/2023/01/chatgpt-cheat-sheet.html
- The Ultimate ChatGPT Guide https://hasantoxr.gumroad.com/l/gpt
- The Art of ChatGPT Prompting: A Guide to Crafting Clear and Effective Prompts https://fka.gumroad.com/l/art-of-chatgpt-prompting
- Prompts Discover the best prompts as rated by FlowGPT users that fit your needs! https://flowgpt.com/prompts

Unlock the full potential of your classroom with 100 effective prompts designed to inspire, engage, and transform the way you teach.

If one's objective is to optimize efficiency and effectiveness by allowing greater focus on the substance and trajectory of ChatGPT conversations rather than the creation of prompts, this book offers a pragmatic and successful resolution. This book offers one hundred fully customizable templates specifically designed for instructional purposes. Using these templates will enable you to effortlessly enhance your educational content. Simply adjust the parameters enclosed in brackets within each template to correspond with your specific pedagogical needs. To elevate your teaching to unprecedented levels of success, immediately enhance your understanding of ChatGPT.

© Miguel Morales-Chan Ph.D

No part of this book may be reproduced in any form without the written permission of the publisher or the author.

Made in United States
Troutdale, OR
08/17/2024

22026283R00060